Table of Contents - Level 3D

Section 1 - Mental Math
   Multiplication and Division WarmUp 1
   Mental Math Drills 8
   Solutions 31

Section 2 - Drills
   More On Fractions 33
   Long Multiplication 51
   More On Powers 57

Section 3 - FUN And GAMES
   Advanced Venn Diagrams 66
   Animal Algebra 77
   Introduction To Algebra 80
   3 and 4 Dice Game 81
   Math Olympiad Trainer 85
   Advanced Roman Numerals 97
   Inroduction to Probability 99

Section 4
   IXL Recommended Exercises 113
   3D Final Assessment 117
   Homework Assignment 122
   Solutions 127

In the Level-3D booklet there is **A LOT** of stuff, but it mostly reviews material we have perviously seen, so I know you will find it easy. This is why many students complete the 3-senior level **REAL FAST**. In mathematics it is great to brush up on concepts we learned to make sure we really, REALLY, know them.

Two ares which need constant reviewing are FRACTIONS, AREA, and PERIMETER. So we will revisit them to make sure they are at our fingertips. Make sure to warm up your PROTRACTOR - we will be measuring quite a few angles. In fact, at the 3-Senior level we MEASURE a lot of other things: WEIGHTS, VOLUMES and DISTANCES. Hoping you will enjoy solving questions as much as we enjoyed making them!

Renert's Bright Minds™ - August 9, 2020

Basic Arithmetic Review

A MIXED bag

Drill 1 ▼

+	405	520	370	709	240
30					
19					
52					
70					
65					

Time:_____   Accuracy: _____ out of 25

Drill 2 ▼

+	235	132	541	623	303
343					
261					
326					
154					
233					

Time:_____   Accuracy: _____ out of 25

Drill 3 ▼

+	352	264	519	326	483
182					
307					
492					
536					
325					

Time:_____   Accuracy: _____ out of 25

Drill 4: Make up a 1000

Multiplication and Division WarmUp

Complete the diagram so that each pair of numbers across from each other adds up to 1000.

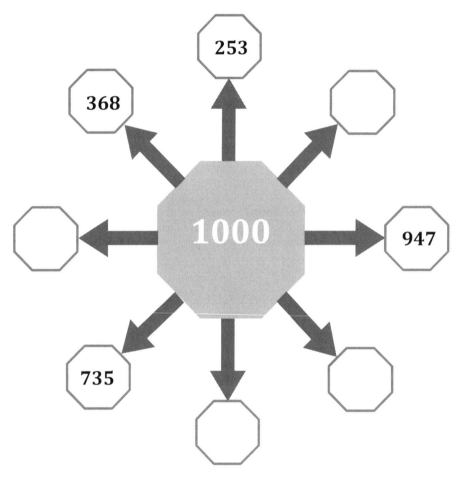

Drill 5:

- 58 − 32 =   27 − 14 =   98 − 53 =
- 76 − 24 =   64 − 51 =   77 − 14 =
- 68 − 11 =   46 − 26 =   87 − 15 =
- 85 − 33 =   85 − 23 =   48 − 17 =

Drill 6:

- 30 – 18 =
- 50 – 35 =
- 40 – 13 =
- 60 – 41 =

60 – 32 =
70 – 43 =
80 – 56 =
90 – 48 =

70 – 29 =
40 – 37 =
50 – 33 =
20 – 17 =

Drill 7:

- 63 – 48 =
- 54 – 37 =
- 51 – 33 =
- 93 – 49 =

86 – 19 =
44 – 25 =
82 – 66 =
93 – 78 =

41 – 38 =
75 – 29 =
46 – 28 =
74 – 57 =

Drill 8:

- 1200 – 400 =
- 5200 – 900 =
- 2300 – 850 =
- 6300 – 720 =

8200 – 1900 =
2050 – 1600 =
8100 – 5300 =
4150 – 3960 =

Drill 9 ▶

X	5	7	8	6	4
9					
3					
7					
6					
8					

Time:_____   Accuracy: _____ out of 25

Drill 10:

- 200 x 50 =
- 400 x 30 =

80 x 90 =
70 x 70 =

300 x 60 =
400 x 80 =

Multiplication and Division WarmUp

- 60 x 400 =   20 x 60 =   60 x 700 =
- 80 x 600 =   50 x 90 =   50 x 800 =

Drill 11:

Example: 124 x 5 = (5 x 100) + (5 x 20) + (5 x 4) = 500 + 100 + 20 = 620

307 x 6 =   420 x 8 =   721 x 5 =

283 x 3 =   2 x 961 =   4 x 479 =

7 x 864 =   7 x 904 =   6 x 324 =

6 x 545 =   345 x 8 =   7 x 219 =

Drill 12: Divide

- 10 ÷ 2 =   12 ÷ 3 =   200 ÷ 50 =
- 21 ÷ 7 =   20 ÷ 10 =   160 ÷ 40 =
- 45 ÷ 5 =   60 ÷ 12 =   640 ÷ 80 =
- 24 ÷ 8 =   72 ÷ 8 =   240 ÷ 40 =
- 63 ÷ 9 =   56 ÷ 7 =   810 ÷ 90 =

- 26 ÷ 8 =   47 ÷ 8 =   245 ÷ 40 =
- 39 ÷ 9 =   29 ÷ 7 =   820 ÷ 90 =
- 33 ÷ 5 =   19 ÷ 2 =   652 ÷ 80 =

Drill 13 ▼

X	2	5	3	6	10
182					
307					
492					
536					
325					

Time:_____   Accuracy: _____ out of 25

Drill 14 ▶

X	235	132	541	623	303
7					
9					
8					
4					
6					

Time:_____   Accuracy: _____ out of 25

Drill 15: Divide (many have remainders)

- $10 \div 3 =$
- $21 \div 8 =$
- $45 \div 6 =$
- $24 \div 9 =$
- $63 \div 10 =$

$12 \div 5 \ =$
$20 \div 18 =$
$60 \div 13 =$
$72 \div 3 \ =$
$78 \div 7 \ =$

$200 \div 30 =$
$160 \div 14 =$
$720 \div 80 =$
$640 \div 100 =$
$800 \div 90 =$

- $260 \div 11 =$
- $139 \div 10 =$
- $313 \div 5 =$

$48 \div 2 =$
$880 \div 80 =$
$880 \div 40 =$

$880 \div 20 =$
$880 \div 10 =$
$880 \div 5 =$

Multiplication and Division WarmUp

Drill 16: Solve by long division

$4 \overline{)236}$ $8 \overline{)397}$ $9 \overline{)518}$

$6 \overline{)744}$ $5 \overline{)632}$ $3 \overline{)496}$

$5 \overline{)621}$ $2 \overline{)794}$ $7 \overline{)802}$

Drill 17: Solve mentally (▶)

- $18 \div 6 =$ $180 \div 6 =$ $180 \div 60 =$
- $28 \div 4 =$ $280 \div 4 =$ $280 \div 40 =$
- $36 \div 6 =$ $360 \div 6 =$ $360 \div 60 =$
- $32 \div 8 =$ $320 \div 8 =$ $320 \div 80 =$
- $49 \div 7 =$ $490 \div 7 =$ $490 \div 70 =$

- $126 \div 6 =$ $804 \div 4 =$ $720 \div 6 =$
- $264 \div 2 =$ $930 \div 3 =$ $960 \div 8 =$
- $618 \div 6 =$ $525 \div 5 =$ $816 \div 4 =$
- $714 \div 7 =$ $416 \div 4 =$ $910 \div 7 =$
- $954 \div 9 =$ $364 \div 4 =$ $294 \div 7 =$

Drill 18: Double these

- 60 _____   80 _____   12 _____   23 _____
- 46 _____   37 _____   79 _____   96 _____
- 160 _____   283 _____   412 ____   523 _____
- 3405 _____   2183 _____   4567 ____   5239 _____

Drill 19: HALF these (▶)

- 60 _____   84 _____   72 _____   38 _____
- 146 _____   156 _____   790 _____   964 _____
- 162 _____   284 _____   412 ____   532 _____
- 2162 _____   1284 _____   1412 ____   1532 _____

Renert's Bright Minds expresses its gratitude to Jack Hope, Barbara and Bob Reys for creating this wonderful resource and allowing our students to use it throughout the program.

Mental Math
in the Middle Grades
Jack A. Hope   Barbara J. Reys   Robert E. Reys

LESSON 28 DOUBLING

Doubling numbers is something we do every day. Here's an easy way to do it in your head:

Double a number by doubling each of its parts. Then add.

TRY THESE IN YOUR HEAD.

Double each number by parts.

1. Double 34
2. Double 81
3. Double 912
4. Double 47
5. Double 29
6. Double 430
7. Double 64
8. Double 75
9. Double 54
10. Double 720

POWER BUILDER A

1. Double 23 = _____
2. Double 62 = _____
3. Double 210 = _____
4. Double 207 = _____
5. Double 45 = _____
6. Double 508 = _____
7. Double 57 = _____
8. Double 98 = _____
9. Double 250 = _____
10. Double 900 = _____
11. Double 42 = _____
12. Double 91 = _____
13. Double 325 = _____
14. Double 36 = _____
15. Double 55 = _____
16. Double 86 = _____
17. Double 64 = _____
18. Double 128 = _____
19. Double 256 = _____
20. Double 512 = _____

THINK IT THROUGH

Think of a number. Double it. Add 6. Divide by 2. Subtract the number you thought of first. Now do the same thing with a new starting number. Can you explain why your answer is always 3?

Copyright © 1987 By Dale Seymour Publications

MENTAL MATH IN THE MIDDLE GRADES — LESSON 28 DOUBLING

POWER BUILDER B

1. Double 43 = _____
2. Double 74 = _____
3. Double 113 = _____
4. Double 16 = _____
5. Double 85 = _____
6. Double 700 = _____
7. Double 87 = _____
8. Double 97 = _____
9. Double 65 = _____
10. Double 840 = _____
11. Double 34 = _____
12. Double 83 = _____
13. Double 424 = _____
14. Double 409 = _____
15. Double 75 = _____
16. Double 27 = _____
17. Double 54 = _____
18. Double 108 = _____
19. Double 216 = _____
20. Double 432 = _____

THINK IT THROUGH

Think of a number. Multiply it by 4. Subtract 8. Divide by 4. Add 2. Now do the same thing with a new starting number. Can you explain your answer?

96

Copyright © 1987 By Dale Seymour Publications

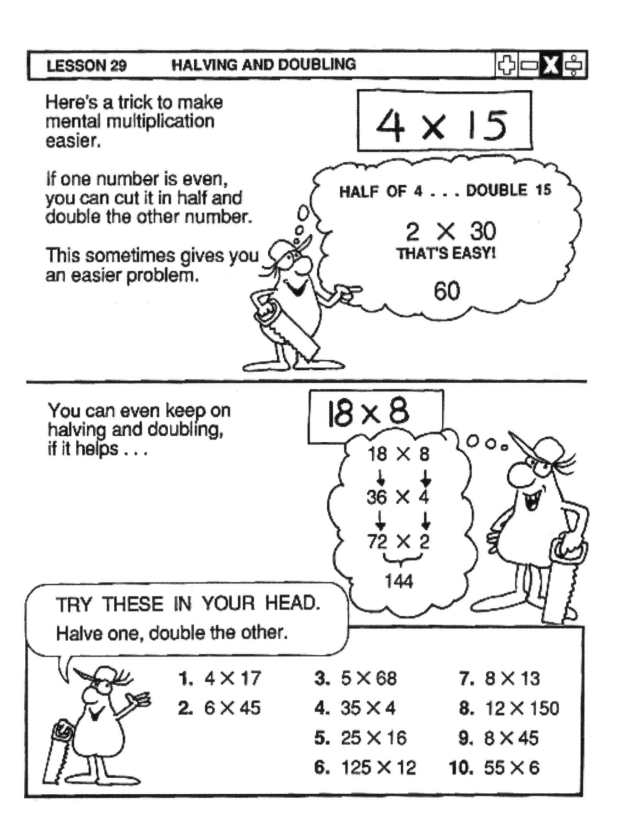

POWER BUILDER A

1. 4 × 13 = _____
2. 6 × 15 = _____
3. 8 × 35 = _____
4. 23 × 4 = _____
5. 35 × 6 = _____
6. 4 × 55 = _____
7. 6 × 65 = _____
8. 8 × 15 = _____
9. 37 × 4 = _____
10. 25 × 6 = _____

11. 14 × 15 = _____
12. 15 × 32 = _____
13. 14 × 25 = _____
14. 18 × 25 = _____
15. 250 × 16 = _____
16. 150 × 6 = _____
17. 150 × 14 = _____
18. 125 × 8 = _____
19. 14 × 35 = _____
20. 12 × 150 = _____

THINK IT THROUGH

Use mental math to decide which of the following equals 64 × 32:
64 × 16   128 × 16
32 × 128   128 × 64

Copyright © 1987 By Dale Seymour Publications

MENTAL MATH IN THE MIDDLE GRADES   LESSON 29   HALVING AND DOUBLING

POWER BUILDER B

1. 4 × 14 = _____
2. 6 × 25 = _____
3. 8 × 45 = _____
4. 24 × 4 = _____
5. 45 × 6 = _____
6. 4 × 65 = _____
7. 6 × 55 = _____
8. 8 × 55 = _____
9. 47 × 4 = _____
10. 75 × 6 = _____

11. 18 × 15 = _____
12. 16 × 25 = _____
13. 15 × 64 = _____
14. 24 × 15 = _____
15. 225 × 8 = _____
16. 150 × 8 = _____
17. 16 × 12 = _____
18. 125 × 6 = _____
19. 18 × 35 = _____
20. 15 × 120 = _____

THINK IT THROUGH

Use mental math to decide which of the following equals 48 × 144:
24 × 96   24 × 72
96 × 288   96 × 72

LESSON 30 — DIVIDE BY MULTIPLYING

These are all different ways to think about the same division problem.

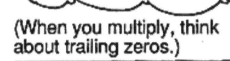

$600 \div 10$ $10\overline{)600}$ $600/10$

600 DIVIDED BY 10

10 DIVIDES 600

Sometimes mental division is easier if you multiply. Think of it this way . . .

10 times WHAT NUMBER equals 600?

10 times $\boxed{60}$ = 600

So . . . $600 \div 10 = 60$

(When you multiply, think about trailing zeros.)

TRY THESE IN YOUR HEAD.
Divide by multiplying.

1. $400 \div 8$
2. $60/10$
3. $5\overline{)100}$
4. $40\overline{)200}$
5. $800 \div 40$
6. $2400 \div 30$
7. $300/3$
8. $70\overline{)3500}$
9. $270 \div 27$
10. $6000/20$

POWER BUILDER A

1. 50 ÷ 5 = _____
2. 60 ÷ 6 = _____
3. 10)80 = _____
4. 30 ÷ 10 = _____
5. 140 ÷ 20 = _____
6. 9)180 = _____
7. 160 ÷ 80 = _____
8. 110 ÷ 11 = _____
9. 80)240 = _____
10. 360 ÷ 9 = _____
11. 400/8 = _____
12. 60)480 = _____
13. 420 ÷ 6 = _____
14. 500/5 = _____
15. 70)630 = _____
16. 540 ÷ 6 = _____
17. 1200/20 = _____
18. 3)2700 = _____
19. 4900 ÷ 7 = _____
20. 6400/80 = _____

THINK IT THROUGH

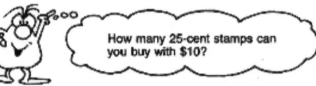

How many 25-cent stamps can you buy with $10?

MENTAL MATH IN THE MIDDLE GRADES   LESSON 30   DIVIDE BY MULTIPLYING

POWER BUILDER B

1. 40 ÷ 8 = _____
2. 70 ÷ 7 = _____
3. 10)90 = _____
4. 50 ÷ 10 = _____
5. 1200 ÷ 20 = _____
6. 7)140 = _____
7. 1200 ÷ 600 = _____
8. 120 ÷ 20 = _____
9. 90)270 = _____
10. 320 ÷ 8 = _____
11. 300/5 = _____
12. 70)420 = _____
13. 480 ÷ 8 = _____
14. 600/6 = _____
15. 90)5400 = _____
16. 630 ÷ 9 = _____
17. 1500/30 = _____
18. 2)1800 = _____
19. 5400 ÷ 6 = _____
20. 8100/9 = _____

THINK IT THROUGH

How many 25-cent stamps can you buy with $100?

100

Student Handbook - Level 3D

LESSON 31 — TACK ON TRAILING ZEROS

Numbers with trailing zeros are easy to divide in your head.

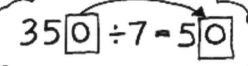

- CUT OFF the trailing zeros.
- DIVIDE the remaining numbers.
- TACK the trailing zeros onto your answer.
- CHECK by multiplying.

Here's how a mental-math pro thinks...

TRY THESE IN YOUR HEAD. Watch the trailing zeros.

1. 120 ÷ 6
2. 1800 ÷ 2
3. 700 ÷ 7
4. 9)720
5. 2)20,000
6. 3600 ÷ 36
7. 7)770
8. 7)7700
9. 2400 ÷ 8
10. 5)2500

POWER BUILDER A

1. 20 ÷ 2 = _____
2. 80 ÷ 4 = _____
3. 90 ÷ 3 = _____
4. 600 ÷ 3 = _____
5. 1200 ÷ 4 = _____
6. 1500 ÷ 5 = _____
7. 8)8000 = _____
8. 4000 ÷ 4 = _____
9. 3)6000 = _____
10. 6000 ÷ 2 = _____

11. 540 ÷ 6 = _____
12. 9)270 = _____
13. 180 ÷ 2 = _____
14. 250 ÷ 5 = _____
15. 7)630 = _____
16. 4900 ÷ 7 = _____
17. 12)1200 = _____
18. 4)20,000 = _____
19. 24,000 ÷ 8 = _____
20. 22,000 ÷ 2 = _____

THINK IT THROUGH

Find the largest 2-digit number that leaves a remainder of 3 when divided by 4.

Copyright © 1987 By Dale Seymour Publications

MENTAL MATH IN THE MIDDLE GRADES LESSON 31 TACK ON TRAILING ZEROS

POWER BUILDER B

1. 60 ÷ 3 = _____
2. 5)50 = _____
3. 80 ÷ 4 = _____
4. 1200 ÷ 2 = _____
5. 4)800 = _____
6. 1800 ÷ 3 = _____
7. 7000 ÷ 7 = _____
8. 1200 ÷ 3 = _____
9. 8000 ÷ 4 = _____
10. 3)9000 = _____

11. 540 ÷ 9 = _____
12. 360 ÷ 4 = _____
13. 3)180 = _____
14. 4)240 = _____
15. 490 ÷ 7 = _____
16. 8)3200 = _____
17. 1300 ÷ 13 = _____
18. 10,000 ÷ 5 = _____
19. 7)28,000 = _____
20. 33,000 ÷ 3 = _____

THINK IT THROUGH

Find the smallest number that does all of the following: leaves a remainder of 1 when divided by 4, leaves a remainder of 2 when divided by 5, and leaves a remainder of 3 when divided by 6.

102

Copyright © 1987 By Dale Seymour Publications

LESSON 32 — CANCELING COMMON ZEROS

DIVIDE IN YOUR HEAD

$400 \div 20$

When both numbers have trailing zeros, you can make the problem easier to do in your head.

$40\cancel{0} \div 2\cancel{0}$

$40 \div 2 = 20$

CANCEL the zeros that the numbers have in common. (In this case, we divide both numbers by 10.)

Remember, don't cancel ALL the trailing zeros. Just cancel the zeros common to both numbers.

TRY THESE IN YOUR HEAD.
Cancel the common zeros.

1. $600 \div 20$
2. $600 \div 300$
3. $8000 \div 2000$
4. $800 \div 20$
5. $1000 \div 20$
6. $9000 \div 30$
7. $3000 \div 200$
8. $5000 \div 50$
9. $1200 \div 60$
10. $1800 \div 200$

POWER BUILDER A

1. 80 ÷ 20 = _____
2. 60 ÷ 20 = _____
3. 90 ÷ 30 = _____
4. 120 ÷ 20 = _____
5. 150 ÷ 30 = _____
6. 270 ÷ 30 = _____
7. 360 ÷ 40 = _____
8. 480 ÷ 80 = _____
9. 500 ÷ 50 = _____
10. 800 ÷ 20 = _____

11. 900 ÷ 30 = _____
12. 1000 ÷ 200 = _____
13. 1000 ÷ 500 = _____
14. 1200 ÷ 200 = _____
15. 1800 ÷ 20 = _____
16. 6400 ÷ 80 = _____
17. 1300 ÷ 20 = _____
18. 4800 ÷ 30 = _____
19. 1360 ÷ 20 = _____
20. 1800 ÷ 40 = _____

THINK IT THROUGH

The state gets a tax of 10 cents for every dollar of gasoline sold. How much money does the state get on gasoline sales of $375,000?

MENTAL MATH IN THE MIDDLE GRADES   LESSON 32   CANCELING COMMON ZEROS

POWER BUILDER B

1. 40 ÷ 20 = _____
2. 80 ÷ 40 = _____
3. 60 ÷ 30 = _____
4. 140 ÷ 20 = _____
5. 180 ÷ 30 = _____
6. 640 ÷ 80 = _____
7. 480 ÷ 60 = _____
8. 360 ÷ 30 = _____
9. 800 ÷ 80 = _____
10. 2400 ÷ 40 = _____

11. 600 ÷ 20 = _____
12. 800 ÷ 40 = _____
13. 400 ÷ 80 = _____
14. 5000 ÷ 500 = _____
15. 7000 ÷ 70 = _____
16. 4800 ÷ 20 = _____
17. 3600 ÷ 30 = _____
18. 5600 ÷ 400 = _____
19. 8400 ÷ 70 = _____
20. 7500 ÷ 500 = _____

THINK IT THROUGH

The state gets a tax of 15 cents for every dollar of gasoline sold. How much money does the state get on sales of $450,000?

LESSON 33 — BREAKING UP THE DIVIDEND

For mental division, you can simplify a problem like this one.

Here's how . . .

Break up the dividend into parts that are easily divided.

- **BREAK UP** 126 into 120 and 6.
- **DIVIDE** both parts by 3.
- **ADD** the answers.
- **CHECK** by multiplying.

$$12{,}6 \div 3$$
$$120 \div 3 = 40$$
$$6 \div 3 = 2$$
$$40 + 2 = 42$$
$$3 \times 42 = 126$$

You might see it in your mind this way . . .

START AT THE LEFT

$$3\overline{)12{,}6} = 42$$

TRY THESE IN YOUR HEAD. Break up the dividend.

1. 44 ÷ 2
2. 63 ÷ 3
3. 648 ÷ 2
4. 168 ÷ 8
5. 324 ÷ 4
6. 525 ÷ 5
7. 287 ÷ 7
8. 248 ÷ 4
9. 455 ÷ 5
10. 918 ÷ 9

Mental Math Drills

POWER BUILDER A

1. 22 ÷ 2 = _____
2. 46 ÷ 2 = _____
3. 36 ÷ 3 = _____
4. 48 ÷ 4 = _____
5. 77 ÷ 7 = _____
6. 64 ÷ 2 = _____
7. 124 ÷ 2 = _____
8. 168 ÷ 8 = _____
9. 212 ÷ 2 = _____
10. 303 ÷ 3 = _____

11. 105 ÷ 5 = _____
12. 108 ÷ 2 = _____
13. 515 ÷ 5 = _____
14. 270 ÷ 3 = _____
15. 639 ÷ 3 = _____
16. 246 ÷ 2 = _____
17. 648 ÷ 6 = _____
18. 816 ÷ 8 = _____
19. 5005 ÷ 5 = _____
20. 2424 ÷ 4 = _____

THINK IT THROUGH

What is the remainder when you divide the sum of 90 + 91 + 92 + 93 + 94 + 95 + 96 + 97 + 98 by 9? (Look for a shortcut!)

Copyright © 1987 By Dale Seymour Publications

MENTAL MATH IN THE MIDDLE GRADES   LESSON 33   BREAKING UP THE DIVIDEND

POWER BUILDER B

1. 28 ÷ 2 = _____
2. 68 ÷ 2 = _____
3. 77 ÷ 7 = _____
4. 86 ÷ 2 = _____
5. 39 ÷ 3 = _____
6. 146 ÷ 2 = _____
7. 147 ÷ 7 = _____
8. 155 ÷ 5 = _____
9. 333 ÷ 3 = _____
10. 124 ÷ 4 = _____

11. 126 ÷ 6 = _____
12. 714 ÷ 7 = _____
13. 404 ÷ 4 = _____
14. 640 ÷ 2 = _____
15. 848 ÷ 4 = _____
16. 749 ÷ 7 = _____
17. 918 ÷ 9 = _____
18. 248 ÷ 4 = _____
19. 8008 ÷ 8 = _____
20. 3636 ÷ 6 = _____

THINK IT THROUGH

What is the remainder when you divide the sum of 52 + 53 + 54 + 55 + 56 + 57 + 58 by 10? (Look for a shortcut!)

106

Copyright © 1987 By Dale Seymour Publications

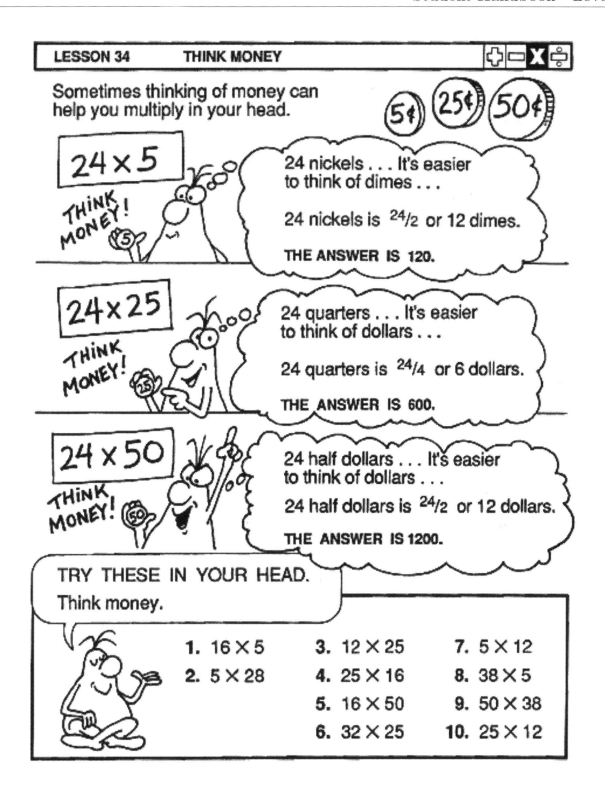

POWER BUILDER A

1. 12 × 5 = _____
2. 5 × 18 = _____
3. 14 × 50 = _____
4. 28 × 25 = _____
5. 5 × 88 = _____
6. 12 × 50 = _____
7. 5 × 48 = _____
8. 64 × 50 = _____
9. 25 × 32 = _____
10. 5 × 36 = _____

11. 26 × 50 = _____
12. 50 × 36 = _____
13. 25 × 64 = _____
14. 56 × 5 = _____
15. 54 × 50 = _____
16. 25 × 240 = _____
17. 50 × 220 = _____
18. 25 × 44 = _____
19. 25 × 180 = _____
20. 5 × 222 = _____

THINK IT THROUGH

An ice machine makes 50 ice cubes every hour. How many cubes can it make in a day?

Copyright © 1987 By Dale Seymour Publications

MENTAL MATH IN THE MIDDLE GRADES — LESSON 34 THINK MONEY

POWER BUILDER B

1. 14 × 5 = _____
2. 5 × 12 = _____
3. 18 × 50 = _____
4. 48 × 25 = _____
5. 5 × 44 = _____
6. 28 × 50 = _____
7. 5 × 64 = _____
8. 48 × 50 = _____
9. 36 × 25 = _____
10. 5 × 32 = _____

11. 22 × 50 = _____
12. 50 × 120 = _____
13. 25 × 88 = _____
14. 54 × 5 = _____
15. 56 × 50 = _____
16. 25 × 280 = _____
17. 50 × 140 = _____
18. 25 × 12 = _____
19. 25 × 220 = _____
20. 5 × 444 = _____

THINK IT THROUGH

An ice machine makes 25 ice cubes every hour. How many cubes can it make in a week?

Copyright © 1987 By Dale Seymour Publications

LESSON 35	SEARCHING FOR COMPATIBLES

MULTIPLY IN YOUR HEAD

$5 \times 7 \times 5 \times 8 \times 2 \times 2$

If you tried to do this problem one step at a time, you would bog down pretty quickly.

5 times 7 is 35, times 5 is . . . too hard!

Make your job easier!
Look for compatible pairs.

10

$5 \times 7 \times 5 \times 8 \times 2 \times 2$

10

Then rearrange the factors to make them easy to multiply in your head.

$7 \times 8 \times 10 \times 10$

$56 \times 100 = 5600$

TRY THESE IN YOUR HEAD.

Look for compatible pairs.

1. $2 \times 7 \times 5$
2. $2 \times 11 \times 15$
3. $4 \times 8 \times 50$
4. $4 \times 9 \times 25$

5. $6 \times 9 \times 500$
6. $400 \times 13 \times 5$
7. $25 \times 5 \times 4 \times 5$
8. $8 \times 4 \times 3 \times 250$
9. $35 \times 8 \times 2 \times 25$
10. $15 \times 3 \times 2 \times 2 \times 15$

POWER BUILDER A

1. 5 × 3 × 4 = _____
2. 2 × 12 × 5 = _____
3. 2 × 3 × 15 = _____
4. 15 × 5 × 4 = _____
5. 20 × 7 × 5 = _____
6. 2 × 7 × 5 × 6 = _____
7. 15 × 7 × 2 × 3 = _____
8. 6 × 25 × 5 × 4 = _____
9. 11 × 2 × 4 × 25 = _____
10. 25 × 5 × 4 × 4 = _____
11. 15 × 3 × 3 × 2 = _____
12. 4 × 4 × 15 × 5 = _____
13. 5 × 5 × 9 × 2 = _____
14. 5 × 7 × 5 × 4 = _____
15. 9 × 5 × 3 × 4 = _____
16. 13 × 2 × 3 × 5 = _____
17. 5 × 7 × 7 × 2 = _____
18. 5 × 5 × 7 × 2 = _____
19. 11 × 2 × 3 × 5 = _____
20. 9 × 50 × 8 × 2 = _____

THINK IT THROUGH

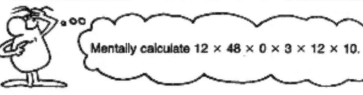

Mentally calculate 12 × 48 × 0 × 3 × 12 × 10.

Copyright © 1987 By Dale Seymour Publications

MENTAL MATH IN THE MIDDLE GRADES   LESSON 35   SEARCHING FOR COMPATIBLES

POWER BUILDER B

1. 4 × 6 × 5 = _____
2. 2 × 9 × 5 = _____
3. 15 × 7 × 2 = _____
4. 4 × 9 × 15 = _____
5. 5 × 3 × 12 = _____
6. 6 × 2 × 3 × 5 = _____
7. 11 × 2 × 5 × 6 = _____
8. 3 × 4 × 25 × 9 = _____
9. 12 × 25 × 3 × 4 = _____
10. 4 × 5 × 25 × 4 = _____
11. 2 × 3 × 5 × 11 = _____
12. 9 × 5 × 8 × 2 = _____
13. 5 × 3 × 2 × 9 = _____
14. 7 × 5 × 3 × 4 = _____
15. 15 × 4 × 5 × 5 = _____
16. 11 × 5 × 5 × 8 = _____
17. 9 × 5 × 20 × 4 = _____
18. 25 × 9 × 5 × 4 = _____
19. 50 × 9 × 2 × 4 = _____
20. 500 × 7 × 3 × 2 = _____

THINK IT THROUGH

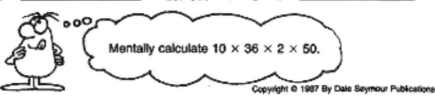

Mentally calculate 10 × 36 × 2 × 50.

110

Copyright © 1987 By Dale Seymour Publications

LESSON 36 — MAKE-YOUR-OWN COMPATIBLE FACTORS

Here's a trick that can simplify mental multiplication . . .

Rearrange one or both of the numbers.

Your aim is to find compatible pairs.

24×25

24×25
$6 \times 4 \times 25$
$6 \times \boxed{4} \times \boxed{25}$ COMPATIBLE!
$6 \times 100 = 600$

Can you find a different way to rearrange 24×25?

TRY THESE IN YOUR HEAD.
Rearrange to find compatible pairs.

1. 8×15
2. 15×24
3. 15×16
4. 36×50
5. 48×15
6. 24×500
7. 12×15
8. 18×500
9. 12×35
10. 15×26

POWER BUILDER A

1. 4 × 35 = _____
2. 4 × 45 = _____
3. 15 × 14 = _____
4. 24 × 15 = _____
5. 15 × 18 = _____
6. 12 × 25 = _____
7. 5 × 24 = _____
8. 8 × 25 = _____
9. 5 × 32 = _____
10. 25 × 16 = _____

11. 22 × 15 = _____
12. 25 × 18 = _____
13. 45 × 16 = _____
14. 15 × 36 = _____
15. 35 × 12 = _____
16. 60 × 25 = _____
17. 55 × 40 = _____
18. 45 × 80 = _____
19. 25 × 180 = _____
20. 450 × 8 = _____

THINK IT THROUGH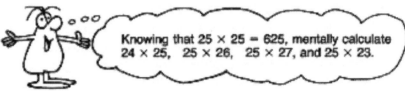

Knowing that 25 × 25 = 625, mentally calculate 24 × 25, 25 × 26, 25 × 27, and 25 × 23.

Copyright © 1987 By Dale Seymour Publications

MENTAL MATH IN THE MIDDLE GRADES   LESSON 36   MAKE-YOUR-OWN COMPATIBLE FACTORS

POWER BUILDER B

1. 6 × 25 = _____
2. 35 × 6 = _____
3. 55 × 4 = _____
4. 6 × 45 = _____
5. 45 × 8 = _____
6. 6 × 55 = _____
7. 45 × 8 = _____
8. 8 × 25 = _____
9. 15 × 22 = _____
10. 25 × 14 = _____

11. 25 × 18 = _____
12. 25 × 28 = _____
13. 45 × 12 = _____
14. 15 × 26 = _____
15. 35 × 14 = _____
16. 40 × 35 = _____
17. 50 × 24 = _____
18. 250 × 16 = _____
19. 40 × 450 = _____
20. 15 × 180 = _____

THINK IT THROUGH

Knowing that 50 × 50 = 2500, mentally calculate 49 × 50, 50 × 51, 48 × 50, and 50 × 52.

112

Copyright © 1987 By Dale Seymour Publications

UNIT FOUR REVIEW   (CLASS DISCUSSION)

Mental Math Techniques
• HALVE ONE, DOUBLE THE OTHER.   4 × 215 = ?   18 × 25 = ?
• TACK ON TRAILING ZEROS.   4200 ÷ 6 = ?
• CANCEL COMMON ZEROS.   27,000 ÷ 300 = ?
• BREAK UP THE DIVIDEND.   1664 ÷ 8 = ?
• THINK MONEY.   16 × 5 = ?   9 × 25 = ?
• SEARCH FOR COMPATIBLES.   50 × 5 × 2 × 4 = ?
• MAKE YOUR OWN COMPATIBLES.   28 × 25 = 4 × 7 × 25 = ?

Do the problems below in your head. Tell which techniques you find useful for each one.

1. 5 × 64
2. 1800 ÷ 200
3. 6 × 2 × 5 × 4
4. 6 × 45
5. 515 ÷ 5
6. 15 × 22
7. 5400/9
8. 50 × 28
9. 3 × 25 × 2 × 4
10. 4000 ÷ 8

Talk about each problem below. What's an easy way to do it in your head? Tell how you would think it through.

1. 56 × 25
2. 260 ÷ 13
3. 4422 ÷ 11
4. 36 × 5
5. 8 × 45
6. 36,000 ÷ 600
7. 14 × 15
8. 3570 ÷ 7
9. 25 × 16
10. 150 × 4 × 2 × 30
11. 5600 ÷ 70
12. 120 × 8

MENTAL MATH PROGRESS TEST

**UNIT FOUR
LESSONS 28–36**

1. Double 33 = _____
2. 217 ÷ 7 = _____
3. 4 × 6 × 50 = _____
4. 60)4200 = _____
5. 25 × 24 = _____
6. 8000 ÷ 20 = _____
7. 5400/6 = _____
8. 45 × 5 × 2 × 2 = _____
9. 12 × 15 = _____
10. 240 ÷ 8 = _____
11. 8 × 24 = _____
12. 8000 ÷ 4 = _____
13. 500 × 26 = _____
14. 621/3 = _____
15. 18 × 8 = _____
16. Double 54 = _____
17. 12 × 25 = _____
18. 600 ÷ 30 = _____
19. 40)1200 = _____
20. 35 × 12 = _____
21. 6300 ÷ 9 = _____
22. 50 × 42 = _____
23. Double 95 = _____
24. 50 × 46 = _____
25. 6000 ÷ 20 = _____

26. 44 × 25 = _____
27. 35)3500 = _____
28. 45 × 6 = _____
29. 4 × 25 × 36 = _____
30. 369 ÷ 9 = _____
31. 8 × 35 = _____
32. 200/5 = _____
33. 40 × 5 × 0 × 6 = _____
34. 444 ÷ 4 = _____
35. Double 29 = _____
36. 11 × 5 × 2 × 9 = _____
37. Double 535 = _____
38. 5 × 48 = _____
39. 1800 ÷ 20 = _____
40. 16 × 15 = _____

MENTAL MATH CUMULATIVE TEST **FORM A**

1. 43 + 35 = _____
2. 68 + 32 = _____
3. 859 − 159 = _____
4. 28 + 75 = _____
5. 328 ÷ 4 = _____
6. 40 × 6 × 5 = _____
7. 3800 ÷ 10 = _____
8. 5 × 125 = _____
9. 6 × 55 = _____
10. 265 − 98 = _____
11. 80 − 24 = _____
12. 25 × 14 × 4 = _____
13. 357 + 299 = _____
14. 2000 ÷ 50 = _____
15. Double 84 = _____
16. 8 × $1.99 = _____
17. 7 × 16 = _____
18. 300 × 40 = _____
19. 5)515 = _____
20. 47 + 29 = _____
21. 5 × 54 = _____
22. 80 − 50 + 30 − 20 = _____
23. 50 × 22 = _____
24. 470 − 300 = _____
25. 2800/70 = _____
26. 55 + 29 = _____
27. 25 × 28 = _____

28. 325 + 25 + 75 = _____
29. 460 + 70 = _____
30. 8 × 99 = _____
31. 48 − 23 = _____
32. 24 × 15 = _____
33. 2600 ÷ 26 = _____
34. 165 + 19 = _____
35. 4000 × 100 = _____
36. 2 × 27 × 5 = _____
37. Double 741 = _____
38. 7000 − 4000 − 300 = _____
39. 4 × 821 = _____
40. 6140 + 500 + 2000 = _____
41. 50 × 38 = _____
42. 200)1800 = _____
43. 8 × 600 = _____
44. $20.00 − $11.98 = _____
45. 75 + 85 + 25 + 2000 = _____
46. 7 × 698 = _____
47. 3 × 74 = _____
48. 426 + 75 = _____
49. 4250 + 30 + 600 = _____
50. 8000 ÷ 2 = _____

MENTAL MATH CUMULATIVE TEST FORM B

1. 34 + 52 = _____
2. 47 + 53 = _____
3. 947 − 247 = _____
4. 28 + 175 = _____
5. 426 ÷ 6 = _____
6. 40 × 8 × 5 = _____
7. 5200 ÷ 10 = _____
8. 8 × 125 = _____
9. 6 × 65 = _____
10. 475 − 98 = _____
11. 11 × 10 = _____
12. 25 × 18 × 4 = _____
13. 463 + 299 = _____
14. 1000 ÷ 50 = _____
15. Double 74 = _____
16. 6 × $4.99 = _____
17. 9 × 16 = _____
18. 500 × 70 = _____
19. 5)‾525 = _____
20. 1000 × 5000 = _____
21. 5 × 48 = _____
22. 90 − 40 + 30 − 20 = _____
23. 50 × 14 = _____

24. 390 − 200 = _____
25. 2700/30 = _____
26. 45 + 37 = _____
27. 25 × 36 = _____
28. 125 + 25 + 75 = _____
29. 590 + 80 = _____
30. 7 × 99 = _____
31. 58 − 24 = _____
32. 24 × 15 = _____
33. 4700 ÷ 47 = _____
34. 155 + 19 = _____
35. 3000 × 100 = _____
36. 2 × 26 × 5 = _____
37. Double 253 = _____
38. 8000 − 6000 − 300 = _____
39. 3 × 623 = _____
40. 3230 + 400 + 5000 = _____
41. 50 × 28 = _____
42. 200)‾16,000 = _____
43. 9 × 700 = _____
44. $20.00 − $13.98 = _____
45. 25 + 95 + 75 + 10 = _____
46. 8 × 798 = _____
47. 5 × 26 = _____
48. 326 + 75 = _____
49. 5420 + 50 + 300 = _____
50. 6000 ÷ 2 = _____

SOLUTIONS to MENTAL MATH DRILLS

LESSON 28

Power Builder A 1. 46 2. 124 3. 420 4. 414 5. 90
6. 1016 7. 114 8. 196 9. 500 10. 1800 11. 84
12. 182 13. 650 14. 72 15. 110 16. 172 17. 128
18. 256 19. 512 20. 1024
Think It Through: Let x = any number. Then
$$\frac{2x + 6}{2} - x = 3.$$

Power Builder B 1. 86 2. 148 3. 226 4. 32 5. 170
6. 1400 7. 174 8. 194 9. 130 10. 1680 11. 68
12. 166 13. 848 14. 818 15. 150 16. 54 17. 108
18. 216 19. 432 20. 864
Think It Through: Answer is always the starting number.
Let x = any number. Then $\frac{4x - 8}{4} + 2 - x$.

LESSON 29

Power Builder A 1. 52 2. 90 3. 280 4. 92 5. 210
6. 220 7. 390 8. 120 9. 148 10. 150 11. 210
12. 480 13. 350 14. 450 15. 4000 16. 900 17. 2100
18. 1000 19. 490 20. 1800
Think It Through: 128×16

Power Builder B 1. 56 2. 150 3. 360 4. 96 5. 270
6. 260 7. 330 8. 440 9. 188 10. 450 11. 270
12. 400 13. 960 14. 360 15. 1800 16. 1200
17. 192 18. 750 19. 630 20. 1800
Think It Through: 96×72

LESSON 30

Power Builder A 1. 10 2. 10 3. 8 4. 3 5. 7 6. 20
7. 2 8. 10 9. 3 10. 40 11. 50 12. 8 13. 70
14. 100 15. 9 16. 90 17. 60 18. 900 19. 700
20. 80
Think It Through: 40 stamps

Power Builder B 1. 5 2. 10 3. 9 4. 5 5. 60 6. 20
7. 2 8. 6 9. 3 10. 40 11. 60 12. 6 13. 60 14. 100
15. 60 16. 70 17. 50 18. 900 19. 900 20. 900
Think It Through: 400 stamps

LESSON 31

Power Builder A 1. 10 2. 20 3. 30 4. 200 5. 300
6. 300 7. 1000 8. 1000 9. 2000 10. 3000 11. 90
12. 30 13. 90 14. 50 15. 90 16. 700 17. 100
18. 5000 19. 3000 20. 11,000
Think It Through: 99

Power Builder B 1. 20 2. 10 3. 20 4. 600 5. 200
6. 600 7. 1000 8. 400 9. 2000 10. 3000 11. 60
12. 90 13. 60 14. 60 15. 70 16. 400 17. 100
18. 2000 19. 4000 20. 11,000
Think It Through: 57

LESSON 32

Power Builder A 1. 4 2. 3 3. 3 4. 6 5. 5 6. 9
7. 9 8. 6 9. 10 10. 40 11. 30 12. 5 13. 2 14. 6
15. 90 16. 80 17. 65 18. 160 19. 68 20. 45
Think It Through: $37,500

Power Builder B 1. 2 2. 2 3. 2 4. 7 5. 6 6. 8
7. 8 8. 12 9. 10 10. 60 11. 30 12. 20 13. 5
14. 10 15. 100 16. 240 17. 120 18. 14 19. 120
20. 15
Think It Through: $67,500

LESSON 33

Power Builder A 1. 11 2. 23 3. 12 4. 12 5. 11
6. 32 7. 62 8. 21 9. 106 10. 101 11. 21 12. 54
13. 103 14. 90 15. 213 16. 123 17. 108 18. 102
19. 1001 20. 606
Think It Through: 0

Power Builder B 1. 14 2. 34 3. 11 4. 43 5. 13
6. 73 7. 21 8. 31 9. 111 10. 31 11. 21 12. 102
13. 101 14. 320 15. 212 16. 107 17. 102 18. 62
19. 1001 20. 606
Think It Through: 5

LESSON 34

Power Builder A 1. 60 2. 90 3. 700 4. 700 5. 440
6. 600 7. 240 8. 3200 9. 800 10. 180 11. 1300
12. 1800 13. 1600 14. 280 15. 2700 16. 6000
17. 11,000 18. 1100 19. 4500 20. 1110
Think It Through: 1200 cubes

Power Builder B 1. 70 2. 60 3. 900 4. 1200 5. 220
6. 1400 7. 320 8. 2400 9. 900 10. 160 11. 1100
12. 6000 13. 2200 14. 270 15. 2800 16. 7000
17. 7000 18. 300 19. 5500 20. 2220
Think It Through: 4200 cubes

LESSON 35

Power Builder A 1. 60 2. 120 3. 90 4. 300 5. 700
6. 420 7. 630 8. 3000 9. 2200 10. 2000 11. 270
12. 1200 13. 450 14. 700 15. 540 16. 390 17. 490
18. 350 19. 330 20. 7200
Think It Through: 0

Power Builder B 1. 120 2. 90 3. 210 4. 540 5. 180
6. 180 7. 660 8. 2700 9. 3600 10. 2000 11. 330
12. 720 13. 270 14. 420 15. 1500 16. 2200
17. 3600 18. 4500 19. 3600 20. 21,000
Think It Through: 36,000

LESSON 36

Power Builder A 1. 140 2. 180 3. 210 4. 360
5. 270 6. 300 7. 120 8. 200 9. 160 10. 400
11. 330 12. 450 13. 720 14. 540 15. 420 16. 1500
17. 2200 18. 3600 19. 4500 20. 3600
Think It Through: 600; 650; 675; 575

Power Builder B 1. 150 2. 210 3. 220 4. 270
5. 360 6. 330 7. 360 8. 200 9. 330 10. 350
11. 450 12. 700 13. 540 14. 390 15. 490 16. 1400
17. 1200 18. 4000 19. 18,000 20. 2700
Think It Through: 2450; 2550; 2400; 2600

UNIT FOUR PROGRESS TEST

1. 66 2. 31 3. 1200 4. 70 5. 600 6. 400 7. 900
8. 900 9. 180 10. 30 11. 192 12. 2000 13. 13,000
14. 207 15. 144 16. 108 17. 300 18. 20 19. 30
20. 420 21. 700 22. 2100 23. 190 24. 2300 25. 300
26. 1100 27. 100 28. 270 29. 3600 30. 41 31. 280
32. 40 33. 0 34. 111 35. 58 36. 990 37. 1070
38. 240 39. 90 40. 240

Solutions

CUMULATIVE TEST, FORM A

1. 78 2. 100 3. 700 4. 103 5. 82 6. 1200 7. 380
8. 625 9. 330 10. 167 11. 56 12. 1400 13. 656
14. 40 15. 168 16. $15.92 17. 112 18. 12,000
19. 103 20. 76 21. 270 22. 40 23. 1100 24. 170
25. 40 26. 84 27. 700 28. 425 29. 530 30. 792
31. 25 32. 360 33. 100 34. 184 35. 400,000
36. 270 37. 1482 38. 2700 39. 3284 40. 8640
41. 1900 42. 9 43. 4800 44. $8.02 45. 2185
46. 4886 47. 222 48. 501 49. 4880 50. 4000

CUMULATIVE TEST, FORM B

1. 86 2. 100 3. 700 4. 203 5. 71 6. 1600 7. 520
8. 1000 9. 390 10. 377 11. 110 12. 1800 13. 762
14. 20 15. 148 16. $29.94 17. 144 18. 35,000
19. 105 20. 5,000,000 21. 240 22. 60 23. 700
24. 190 25. 90 26. 82 27. 900 28. 225 29. 670
30. 693 31. 34 32. 360 33. 100 34. 174
35. 300,000 36. 260 37. 506 38. 1700 39. 1869
40. 8630 41. 1400 42. 80 43. 6300 44. $6.02
45. 205 46. 6384 47. 130 48. 401 49. 5770
50. 3000

More on FRACTIONS: **Equivalent Fractions**

Some fractions, although they "look different", have the exact same value. We call them **EQUIVALENT FRACTIONS**. For example, let's look at the fraction $\frac{1}{2}$:

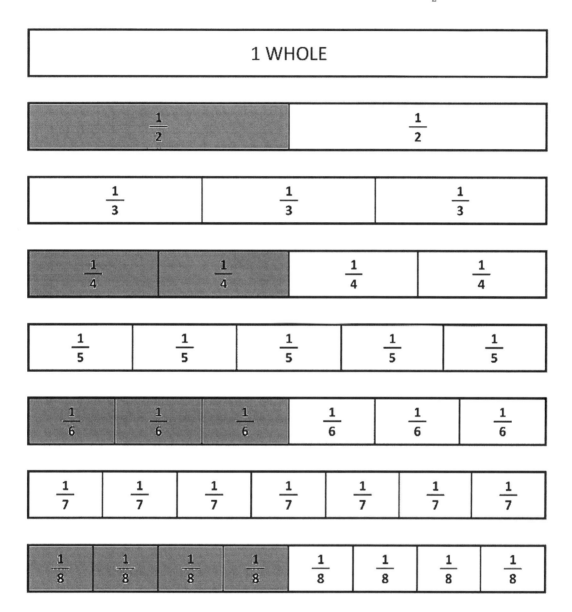

Notice that $\frac{1}{2} = \frac{2}{4} = \frac{3}{6} = \frac{4}{8} = \ldots$ There are many other fractions that are equivalent to $\frac{1}{2}$. Can you find some more? _____

A quick way to construct equivalent fractions is to multiply or divide both the numerator and denominator by the **SAME** number. For example: $\frac{1}{4}$ and $\frac{6}{24}$ are

More On Fractions

equivalent fractions; I can get from $\frac{1}{4}$ to $\frac{6}{24}$ by multiplying both the numerator and denominator by 6.

I can go backwards to get from $\frac{6}{24}$ to $\frac{1}{4}$ by dividing both the numerator and denominator by 6. In order to get equivalent fractions, we multiply or divide the numerator and denominator by the SAME number

Sometimes, working with smaller numbers is easier. We do this by putting our fractions to its **lowest possible equivalent fraction** (that means divide both the numerator and denominator by the same number until we can't do it anymore). This process is called "put in simplest form", or "put in lowest terms", or just simply "reduce".

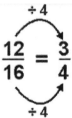

$\frac{3}{4}$ is the simplest form of $\frac{12}{16}$

Notice how $\frac{3}{4}$ is the simplest possible form of $\frac{12}{16}$. We cannot reduce it anymore.

In each line write two more fractions that are equivalent to the ones given:

Student Handbook - Level 3D

a) $\dfrac{7}{10}$ $\dfrac{14}{20}$ $\dfrac{21}{30}$

b) $\dfrac{3}{9}$ $\dfrac{6}{18}$ $\dfrac{9}{27}$

c) $\dfrac{6}{7}$ $\dfrac{12}{14}$ $\dfrac{18}{21}$

d) $\dfrac{4}{8}$ $\dfrac{8}{16}$ $\dfrac{12}{24}$

e) $\dfrac{1}{3}$ $\dfrac{2}{6}$ $\dfrac{3}{9}$

More On Fractions

Continue the pattern in each line to make more equivalent fractions:

a) $\quad \dfrac{2}{4} \quad \dfrac{4}{8} \quad \dfrac{6}{12}$

b) $\quad \dfrac{4}{9} \quad \dfrac{8}{18} \quad \dfrac{12}{27}$

c) $\quad \dfrac{2}{5} \quad \dfrac{4}{10} \quad \dfrac{6}{15}$

d) $\quad \dfrac{3}{7} \quad \dfrac{6}{14} \quad \dfrac{9}{21}$

e) $\quad \dfrac{8}{10} \quad \dfrac{16}{20} \quad \dfrac{24}{30}$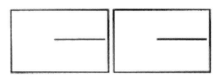

In each line, put a ✓ on all the fractions that are equivalent to the one on the left:

a) $\dfrac{5}{7}$ $\dfrac{25}{35}$ $\dfrac{13}{56}$ $\dfrac{3}{77}$ $\dfrac{20}{42}$ $\dfrac{4}{14}$

b) $\dfrac{4}{6}$ $\dfrac{12}{18}$ $\dfrac{8}{12}$ $\dfrac{39}{66}$ $\dfrac{19}{54}$ $\dfrac{32}{48}$

c) $\dfrac{2}{10}$ $\dfrac{17}{100}$ $\dfrac{11}{80}$ $\dfrac{5}{30}$ $\dfrac{12}{60}$ $\dfrac{8}{40}$

d) $\dfrac{2}{5}$ $\dfrac{12}{30}$ $\dfrac{6}{15}$ $\dfrac{12}{40}$ $\dfrac{22}{55}$ $\dfrac{10}{25}$

e) $\dfrac{4}{9}$ $\dfrac{20}{45}$ $\dfrac{12}{27}$ $\dfrac{16}{54}$ $\dfrac{32}{72}$ $\dfrac{28}{63}$

More On Fractions

In each line, put a ✓ on all the fractions that are equivalent to the one on the left:

a) $\dfrac{5}{6}$ — $\dfrac{25}{30}$ $\dfrac{45}{54}$ $\dfrac{20}{24}$ $\dfrac{25}{48}$ $\dfrac{10}{12}$

b) $\dfrac{5}{10}$ — $\dfrac{50}{100}$ $\dfrac{2}{40}$ $\dfrac{13}{30}$ $\dfrac{55}{110}$ $\dfrac{14}{70}$

c) $\dfrac{7}{9}$ — $\dfrac{5}{63}$ $\dfrac{56}{72}$ $\dfrac{29}{45}$ $\dfrac{14}{18}$ $\dfrac{43}{99}$

d) $\dfrac{3}{5}$ — $\dfrac{7}{30}$ $\dfrac{9}{15}$ $\dfrac{12}{20}$ $\dfrac{33}{55}$ $\dfrac{7}{25}$

e) $\dfrac{4}{8}$ — $\dfrac{9}{24}$ $\dfrac{3}{88}$ $\dfrac{3}{32}$ $\dfrac{17}{80}$ $\dfrac{32}{64}$

Find the missing numerator (the number on top) to make the fractions equivalent:

a) $\dfrac{3}{4} = \dfrac{}{28}$

b) $\dfrac{8}{3} = \dfrac{}{27}$

c) $\dfrac{5}{4} = \dfrac{}{12}$

d) $\dfrac{4}{10} = \dfrac{}{60}$

e) $\dfrac{2}{3} = \dfrac{}{6}$

f) $\dfrac{4}{3} = \dfrac{}{21}$

g) $\dfrac{7}{9} = \dfrac{}{81}$

h) $\dfrac{1}{7} = \dfrac{}{28}$

i) $\dfrac{4}{5} = \dfrac{}{10}$

j) $\dfrac{7}{2} = \dfrac{}{10}$

k) $\dfrac{6}{10} = \dfrac{}{70}$

l) $\dfrac{7}{5} = \dfrac{}{25}$

More On Fractions

Find the missing denominator (the number on bottom) to make the fractions equivalent:

a) $\dfrac{1}{4} = \dfrac{9}{}$

b) $\dfrac{1}{3} = \dfrac{10}{}$

c) $\dfrac{1}{4} = \dfrac{5}{}$

d) $\dfrac{7}{5} = \dfrac{49}{}$

e) $\dfrac{4}{10} = \dfrac{16}{}$

f) $\dfrac{1}{2} = \dfrac{8}{}$

g) $\dfrac{3}{4} = \dfrac{15}{}$

h) $\dfrac{7}{4} = \dfrac{70}{}$

i) $\dfrac{4}{6} = \dfrac{24}{}$

j) $\dfrac{7}{3} = \dfrac{63}{}$

k) $\dfrac{6}{5} = \dfrac{48}{}$

l) $\dfrac{7}{2} = \dfrac{14}{}$

Find the missing number to make the fractions equivalent:

Ex) $\dfrac{8}{10} = \dfrac{40}{50}$

1) $\dfrac{2}{8} = \dfrac{}{32}$

2) $\dfrac{4}{6} = \dfrac{}{48}$

3) $\dfrac{3}{5} = \dfrac{}{45}$

4) $\dfrac{1}{2} = \dfrac{}{12}$

5) $\dfrac{1}{2} = \dfrac{}{16}$

6) $\dfrac{3}{4} = \dfrac{18}{}$

7) $\dfrac{5}{7} = \dfrac{}{70}$

8) $\dfrac{1}{2} = \dfrac{3}{}$

9) $\dfrac{1}{2} = \dfrac{9}{}$

10) $\dfrac{1}{4} = \dfrac{10}{}$

11) $\dfrac{3}{4} = \dfrac{30}{}$

12) $\dfrac{2}{5} = \dfrac{4}{}$

13) $\dfrac{2}{3} = \dfrac{}{12}$

14) $\dfrac{5}{7} = \dfrac{}{35}$

15) $\dfrac{9}{10} = \dfrac{72}{}$

16) $\dfrac{2}{7} = \dfrac{20}{}$

17) $\dfrac{1}{4} = \dfrac{2}{}$

18) $\dfrac{4}{6} = \dfrac{}{60}$

19) $\dfrac{8}{9} = \dfrac{80}{}$

20) $\dfrac{5}{10} = \dfrac{}{100}$

More On Fractions

True or False?

Write "True" or "False" in each box:

a) $\dfrac{3}{4} = \dfrac{12}{16}$

b) $\dfrac{4}{3} = \dfrac{32}{24}$

c) $\dfrac{2}{5} = \dfrac{6}{15}$

d) $\dfrac{24}{32} = \dfrac{3}{4}$

e) $\dfrac{56}{32} = \dfrac{7}{4}$

f) $\dfrac{42}{12} = \dfrac{7}{2}$

g) $\dfrac{7}{4} = \dfrac{6}{5}$

h) $\dfrac{7}{4} = \dfrac{1}{2}$

I) $\dfrac{6}{5} = \dfrac{3}{2}$

j) $\dfrac{35}{21} = \dfrac{5}{3}$

k) $\dfrac{5}{9} = \dfrac{15}{27}$

l) $\dfrac{5}{7} = \dfrac{15}{21}$

Equal or not equal?

Write $=$ or $\neq$ in each box

a) $\dfrac{25}{10}$ ☐ $\dfrac{5}{2}$ b) $\dfrac{6}{9}$ ☐ $\dfrac{24}{36}$

c) $\dfrac{6}{8}$ ☐ $\dfrac{15}{40}$ d) $\dfrac{4}{8}$ ☐ $\dfrac{9}{24}$

e) $\dfrac{5}{7}$ ☐ $\dfrac{18}{21}$ f) $\dfrac{8}{6}$ ☐ $\dfrac{32}{24}$

g) $\dfrac{1}{8}$ ☐ $\dfrac{15}{40}$ h) $\dfrac{24}{40}$ ☐ $\dfrac{3}{5}$

l) $\dfrac{6}{4}$ ☐ $\dfrac{24}{16}$ j) $\dfrac{20}{15}$ ☐ $\dfrac{2}{6}$

k) $\dfrac{16}{12}$ ☐ $\dfrac{8}{6}$ l) $\dfrac{6}{4}$ ☐ $\dfrac{12}{8}$

More On Fractions

Greater than, Less than, or Equal to?

Write $>$ or $<$ or $=$ in each box

a) $\dfrac{30}{24}$ ☐ $\dfrac{5}{4}$

b) $\dfrac{5}{4}$ ☐ $\dfrac{40}{32}$

c) $\dfrac{7}{6}$ ☐ $\dfrac{14}{12}$

d) $\dfrac{3}{8}$ ☐ $\dfrac{3}{2}$

e) $\dfrac{1}{3}$ ☐ $\dfrac{8}{9}$

f) $\dfrac{7}{3}$ ☐ $\dfrac{8}{7}$

g) $\dfrac{1}{9}$ ☐ $\dfrac{1}{5}$

h) $\dfrac{1}{5}$ ☐ $\dfrac{4}{5}$

i) $\dfrac{1}{6}$ ☐ $\dfrac{4}{5}$

j) $\dfrac{42}{18}$ ☐ $\dfrac{7}{3}$

k) $\dfrac{8}{9}$ ☐ $\dfrac{8}{7}$

l) $\dfrac{6}{5}$ ☐ $\dfrac{6}{5}$

Student Handbook - Level 3D

Less or More than One HALF?

Write beside each fraction $>\frac{1}{2}$ or $<\frac{1}{2}$

Ex) $\dfrac{1}{4}$

1) $\dfrac{2}{10}$

2) $\dfrac{2}{3}$

3) $\dfrac{5}{6}$

4) $\dfrac{4}{5}$

5) $\dfrac{8}{10}$

6) $\dfrac{3}{12}$

7) $\dfrac{1}{10}$

8) $\dfrac{5}{8}$

9) $\dfrac{1}{8}$

10) $\dfrac{2}{5}$

11) $\dfrac{10}{12}$

12) $\dfrac{5}{10}$

13) $\dfrac{3}{4}$

14) $\dfrac{1}{3}$

15) $\dfrac{1}{6}$

16) $\dfrac{3}{6}$

17) $\dfrac{4}{6}$

18) $\dfrac{2}{4}$

19) $\dfrac{7}{10}$

20) $\dfrac{2}{6}$

Renert's Bright Minds™ - August 9, 2020

More On Fractions

REDUCE each fraction to its SIMPLEST FORM

Ex) $\dfrac{10}{40} = \dfrac{1}{4}$

1) $\dfrac{8}{64} = $ ___

2) $\dfrac{40}{64} = $ ___

3) $\dfrac{50}{60} = $ ___

4) $\dfrac{18}{27} = $ ___

5) $\dfrac{3}{24} = $ ___

6) $\dfrac{8}{12} = $ ___

7) $\dfrac{30}{80} = $ ___

8) $\dfrac{8}{48} = $ ___

9) $\dfrac{40}{48} = $ ___

10) $\dfrac{16}{24} = $ ___

11) $\dfrac{24}{32} = $ ___

12) $\dfrac{21}{28} = $ ___

13) $\dfrac{21}{56} = $ ___

14) $\dfrac{9}{36} = $ ___

15) $\dfrac{6}{18} = $ ___

16) $\dfrac{3}{12} = $ ___

17) $\dfrac{5}{40} = $ ___

18) $\dfrac{35}{42} = $ ___

19) $\dfrac{6}{48} = $ ___

20) $\dfrac{20}{30} = $ ___

Solve the following and write your answers on the lines:

1) Write $^{25}/_5$ as a whole number.

2) Write $^{100}/_{10}$ as a whole number.

3) Write $^{30}/_{10}$ as a whole number.

4) Write $^4/_2$ as a whole number.

5) Write $^{54}/_9$ as a whole number.

6) Write $^{24}/_4$ as a whole number.

7) Write $^{40}/_8$ as a whole number.

8) Write $^{35}/_7$ as a whole number.

9) Write $^{30}/_3$ as a whole number.

10) Write $^{63}/_7$ as a whole number.

11) Write 9 as a fraction with 7 in the denominator.

12) Write 5 as a fraction with 6 in the denominator.

13) Write 5 as a fraction with 5 in the denominator.

14) Write 5 as a fraction with 5 in the denominator.

15) Write 2 as a fraction with 3 in the denominator.

16) Write 6 as a fraction with 3 in the denominator.

17) Write 9 as a fraction with 5 in the denominator.

18) Write 6 as a fraction with 10 in the denominator.

19) Write 6 as a fraction with 9 in the denominator.

20) Write 4 as a fraction with 5 in the denominator.

1. _____

2. _____

3. _____

4. _____

5. _____

6. _____

7. _____

8. _____

9. _____

10. _____

11. _____

12. _____

13. _____

14. _____

15. _____

16. _____

17. _____

18. _____

19. _____

20. _____

More On Fractions

REDUCE to simplest form. If IMPROPER, also write as a MIXED NUMBER

a) $\dfrac{16}{14}$ = _____

b) $\dfrac{9}{72}$ = _____

c) $\dfrac{14}{4}$ = _____

d) $\dfrac{18}{60}$ = _____

e) $\dfrac{42}{63}$ = _____

f) $\dfrac{3}{9}$ = _____

g) $\dfrac{56}{72}$ = _____

h) $\dfrac{48}{60}$ = _____

i) $\dfrac{24}{18}$ = _____

j) $\dfrac{27}{54}$ = _____

k) $\dfrac{6}{12}$ = _____

l) $\dfrac{14}{56}$ = _____

REDUCE to simplest form. If IMPROPER, also write as a MIXED NUMBER

a) $\dfrac{58}{20} =$ ___

b) $\dfrac{60}{18} =$ ___

c) $\dfrac{30}{50} =$ ___

d) $\dfrac{12}{28} =$ ___

e) $\dfrac{60}{80} =$ ___

f) $\dfrac{15}{10} =$ ___

g) $\dfrac{10}{6} =$ ___

h) $\dfrac{12}{42} =$ ___

i) $\dfrac{33}{27} =$ ___

j) $\dfrac{21}{27} =$ ___

k) $\dfrac{120}{80} =$ ___

l) $\dfrac{50}{70} =$ ___

More On Fractions

REDUCE to simplest form. If IMPROPER, also also as a MIXED NUMBER

a) $\dfrac{98}{42}$ =

b) $\dfrac{56}{64}$ =

c) $\dfrac{95}{35}$ =

d) $\dfrac{15}{24}$ =

e) $\dfrac{48}{60}$ =

f) $\dfrac{180}{70}$ =

g) $\dfrac{85}{30}$ =

h) $\dfrac{8}{56}$ =

i) $\dfrac{48}{64}$ =

j) $\dfrac{185}{30}$ =

k) $\dfrac{92}{36}$ =

l) $\dfrac{35}{15}$ =

Use the grid paper to perform 2x2 LONG MULTIPLICATION

$$\begin{array}{r} 8\ 2 \\ \times\ 4\ 1 \\ \hline \end{array}$$

$$\begin{array}{r} 4\ 4 \\ \times\ 4\ 2 \\ \hline \end{array}$$

$$\begin{array}{r} 2\ 5 \\ \times\ 1\ 0 \\ \hline \end{array}$$

$$\begin{array}{r} 9\ 3 \\ \times\ 8\ 6 \\ \hline \end{array}$$

$$\begin{array}{r} 7\ 2 \\ \times\ 8\ 7 \\ \hline \end{array}$$

$$\begin{array}{r} 4\ 3 \\ \times\ 1\ 0 \\ \hline \end{array}$$

$$\begin{array}{r} 6\ 2 \\ \times\ 5\ 2 \\ \hline \end{array}$$

$$\begin{array}{r} 5\ 6 \\ \times\ 9\ 6 \\ \hline \end{array}$$

$$\begin{array}{r} 9\ 1 \\ \times\ 4\ 7 \\ \hline \end{array}$$

$$\begin{array}{r} 9\ 4 \\ \times\ 8\ 3 \\ \hline \end{array}$$

$$\begin{array}{r} 7\ 5 \\ \times\ 1\ 3 \\ \hline \end{array}$$

$$\begin{array}{r} 3\ 4 \\ \times\ 9\ 8 \\ \hline \end{array}$$

$$\begin{array}{r} 2\ 3 \\ \times\ 4\ 8 \\ \hline \end{array}$$

$$\begin{array}{r} 4\ 4 \\ \times\ 6\ 2 \\ \hline \end{array}$$

$$\begin{array}{r} 7\ 9 \\ \times\ 9\ 7 \\ \hline \end{array}$$

$$\begin{array}{r} 9\ 9 \\ \times\ 6\ 5 \\ \hline \end{array}$$

Long Multiplication

Solutions

$$
\begin{array}{r}
82 \\
\times\ 41 \\
\hline
82 \\
3280 \\
\hline
3362
\end{array}
\qquad
\begin{array}{r}
44 \\
\times\ 42 \\
\hline
88 \\
1760 \\
\hline
1848
\end{array}
\qquad
\begin{array}{r}
25 \\
\times\ 10 \\
\hline
00 \\
250 \\
\hline
250
\end{array}
\qquad
\begin{array}{r}
93 \\
\times\ 86 \\
\hline
558 \\
7440 \\
\hline
7998
\end{array}
$$

$$
\begin{array}{r}
72 \\
\times\ 87 \\
\hline
504 \\
5760 \\
\hline
6264
\end{array}
\qquad
\begin{array}{r}
43 \\
\times\ 10 \\
\hline
00 \\
430 \\
\hline
430
\end{array}
\qquad
\begin{array}{r}
62 \\
\times\ 52 \\
\hline
124 \\
3100 \\
\hline
3224
\end{array}
\qquad
\begin{array}{r}
56 \\
\times\ 96 \\
\hline
336 \\
5040 \\
\hline
5376
\end{array}
$$

$$
\begin{array}{r}
91 \\
\times\ 47 \\
\hline
637 \\
3640 \\
\hline
4277
\end{array}
\qquad
\begin{array}{r}
94 \\
\times\ 83 \\
\hline
282 \\
7520 \\
\hline
7802
\end{array}
\qquad
\begin{array}{r}
75 \\
\times\ 13 \\
\hline
225 \\
750 \\
\hline
975
\end{array}
\qquad
\begin{array}{r}
34 \\
\times\ 98 \\
\hline
272 \\
3060 \\
\hline
3332
\end{array}
$$

$$
\begin{array}{r}
23 \\
\times\ 48 \\
\hline
184 \\
920 \\
\hline
1104
\end{array}
\qquad
\begin{array}{r}
44 \\
\times\ 62 \\
\hline
88 \\
2640 \\
\hline
2728
\end{array}
\qquad
\begin{array}{r}
79 \\
\times\ 97 \\
\hline
553 \\
7110 \\
\hline
7663
\end{array}
\qquad
\begin{array}{r}
99 \\
\times\ 65 \\
\hline
495 \\
5940 \\
\hline
6435
\end{array}
$$

Use the grid paper to perform 2x3 LONG MULTIPLICATION

	1	8	8
×		1	0

	1	4	1
×		1	4

	4	6	6
×		2	7

	8	7	4
×		6	7

	1	6	9
×		5	2

	6	6	0
×		1	1

	5	4	7
×		1	5

	8	7	4
×		3	5

	4	3	1
×		2	6

	8	9	7
×		2	4

	7	1	0
×		1	7

	3	3	5
×		1	5

	8	0	1
×		6	2

	8	1	1
×		4	4

	1	5	6
×		2	7

	7	0	6
×		7	8

Long Multiplication

Solutions

$$\begin{array}{r} 188 \\ \times\ 10 \\ \hline 000 \\ 1880 \\ \hline 1880 \end{array} \qquad \begin{array}{r} 141 \\ \times\ 14 \\ \hline 564 \\ 1410 \\ \hline 1974 \end{array} \qquad \begin{array}{r} 466 \\ \times\ 27 \\ \hline 3262 \\ 9320 \\ \hline 12582 \end{array} \qquad \begin{array}{r} 874 \\ \times\ 67 \\ \hline 6118 \\ 52440 \\ \hline 58558 \end{array}$$

$$\begin{array}{r} 169 \\ \times\ 52 \\ \hline 338 \\ 8450 \\ \hline 8788 \end{array} \qquad \begin{array}{r} 660 \\ \times\ 11 \\ \hline 660 \\ 6600 \\ \hline 7260 \end{array} \qquad \begin{array}{r} 547 \\ \times\ 15 \\ \hline 2735 \\ 5470 \\ \hline 8205 \end{array} \qquad \begin{array}{r} 874 \\ \times\ 35 \\ \hline 4370 \\ 26220 \\ \hline 30590 \end{array}$$

$$\begin{array}{r} 431 \\ \times\ 26 \\ \hline 2586 \\ 8620 \\ \hline 11206 \end{array} \qquad \begin{array}{r} 897 \\ \times\ 24 \\ \hline 3588 \\ 17940 \\ \hline 21528 \end{array} \qquad \begin{array}{r} 710 \\ \times\ 17 \\ \hline 4970 \\ 7100 \\ \hline 12070 \end{array} \qquad \begin{array}{r} 335 \\ \times\ 15 \\ \hline 1675 \\ 3350 \\ \hline 5025 \end{array}$$

$$\begin{array}{r} 801 \\ \times\ 62 \\ \hline 1602 \\ 48060 \\ \hline 49662 \end{array} \qquad \begin{array}{r} 811 \\ \times\ 44 \\ \hline 3244 \\ 32440 \\ \hline 35684 \end{array} \qquad \begin{array}{r} 156 \\ \times\ 27 \\ \hline 1092 \\ 3120 \\ \hline 4212 \end{array} \qquad \begin{array}{r} 706 \\ \times\ 78 \\ \hline 5648 \\ 49420 \\ \hline 55068 \end{array}$$

Use the grid paper to perform 3x3 LONG MULTIPLICATION

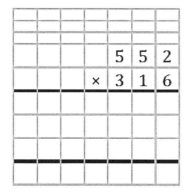
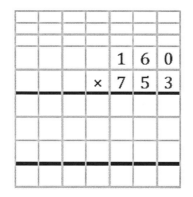

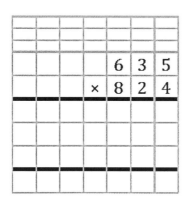
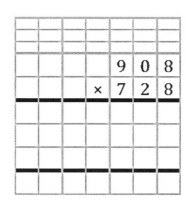
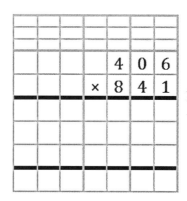

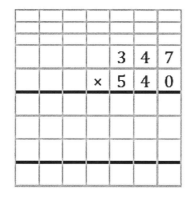
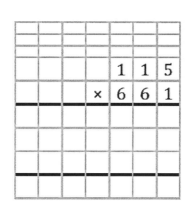

Student Handbook - Level 3D

Long Multiplication

Solutions

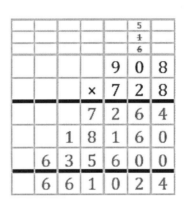

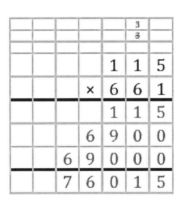

POWERS and EXPONENTS: Quick Review

base $\longrightarrow$ 3^4 = 3 · 3 · 3 · 3

exponent, power

$$2 \times 2 = 2^2 = 4$$
$$2 \times 2 \times 2 = 2^3 = 8$$
$$2 \times 2 \times 2 \times 2 = 2^4 = 16$$
$$2 \times 2 \times 2 \times 2 \times 2 = 2^5 = 32$$
$$2 \times 2 \times 2 \times 2 \times 2 \times 2 = 2^6 = 64$$
$$2 \times 2 \times 2 \times 2 \times 2 \times 2 \times 2 = 2^7 = 128$$

POWERS are used when we multiply a number BY ITSELF. For example, when we multiply 2 by itself five times, instead of writing $2 \times 2 \times 2 \times 2 \times 2$, we can simply write 2^5. This saves us time. In words we say "2 to the power of 5". The number 2 in this case is the BASE, and 5 is the POWER.

Examples:

$2^4 = 2 \times 2 \times 2 \times 2 = $ _____ $10^2 = 10 \times 10 = $ _____ $5^3 = 5 \times 5 \times 5 = $ _____

$3^3 = 3 \times 3 \times 3 = $ _____ $7^2 = 7 \times 7 = $ _____ $8^1 = $ _____

$3^0 = $ _____ $7^0 = $ _____ $8^0 = $ _____

More On Powers

What do we do when the power is ZERO?

LET'S EXPLORE: Continue the patters below:

A. 128, 64, 32, 16, ____, ____, ____, ____

B. 2^7, 2^6, 2^5, 2^4, ____, ____, ____, ____

NOW try these ones:

A. 27, 9, 3, ____, ____, ____, ____

B. 3^3, 3^2, 3^1, 3^0, ____, ____, ____

ANY NUMBER TO THE POWER OF ZERO IS:_____

A. Fill in the correct numbers in the boxes and on the lines

1. $2^{\square} = 8$ 2. $3^{\square} = 9$ 3. $4^{\square} = 64$ 4. $2^{\square} = 32$

5. $5^{\square} = 125$ 6. $6^{\square} = 36$ 7. $7^{\square} = 7$ 8. $8^{\square} = 1$

9. $10^{\square} = 1000$ 10. $\_\_\_^2 = 9$ 11. $\_\_\_^4 = 16$ 12. $\_\_\_^5 = 0$

13. $\_\_\_^1 = 13$ 14. $\_\_\_^3 = 27$ 15. $\_\_\_^0 = 1$ 16. $\_\_\_^2 = 100$

B. Use < or > or = on the lines below

1. 2^{10} _____ 2^8 2. 9^7 _____ 9^9 3. 7^{11} _____ 7^7

4. 3^4 _____ 3^6 6. 1^7 _____ 1^9 6. 0^{11} _____ 7^7

7. 9^1 _____ 7^1 8. 9^0 _____ 7^0 9. 10^1 _____ 1^{10}

Rule 1: $1^x = 1$

Rule 2: $0^x = 0$

Rule 3: $x^0 =$

C. ORDER OF OPERATIONS with POWERS

1. $25+3^2 =$ _____   2. $7+2^3 =$ _____   3. $19-2^4 =$ _____

4. $45-2^5 =$ _____   5. $7 \times 2^3 =$ _____   6. $2 \times 3^2 =$ _____

7. $48 \div 2^3 =$ _____   8. $40 \div 5^3 =$ _____   9. $19 \div 2^0 =$ _____

10. $3 \times 5^2 + 2 \times 3^2 =$ _____   11. $7+4 \times 2^3 =$ _____   12. $50-3 \times 2^4 =$ _____

13. $2 \times 3^2 - 3 \times 2^2 =$ _____   14. $5^1 \times 4^2 - 2^6 =$ _____   15. $3^0 \times 10^2 - 3^2 \times 10^0 =$ _____

16. $(8-5)^2 =$ _____   17. $(11-3 \times 2)^3 =$ _____   18. $(192-2^4)^0 =$ _____

Review: POWERS of 2

More On Powers

Exponential Form	Expanded Form	Actual Value
2^0	1	1
	2	2
2^2	2 x 2	
2^3		8
	2 x 2 x 2 x 2	
2^5	2 x 2 x 2 x 2 x 2	
2^6		64
		128
	2 x 2 x 2 x 2 x 2 x 2 x 2 x 2	
2^9		
2^{10}	2 x 2 x 2 x 2 x 2 x 2 x 2 x 2 x 2 x 2	

Review: PERFECT SQUARES

Exponential Form	Expanded Form	Actual Value
0^2	0 x 0	0
1^2		
2^2		
3^2		
4^2		
5^2		
6^2		
7^2		

8^2		
9^2		
10^2	10 x 10	100

Review: PERFECT CUBES

Exponential Form	Expanded Form	Actual Value
0^3		
1^3		
2^3		
3^3		
4^3		
5^3	5 x 5 x 5	125
6^3		
7^3		
8^3		
9^3		
10^3		

More On Powers

POWERS of 10

Exponential Form	Expanded Form	Actual Value
10^0		
10^1		
10^2		
10^3		
10^4		
10^5	10x10x10x10x10	
10^6		
10^7		
10^8	10x10x10x10x10x10x10x10	
10^9	10x10x10x10x10x10x10x10x10	
10^{10}	10x10x10x10x10x10x10x10x10x10	

Some HUGE Numbers

- 300,000,000,000 STARS IN THE MILKY WAY
- 238,855 MILES DISTANCE TO THE MOON
- 13,800,000,000 YEARS AGO THE BIG BANG
- 37,200,000,000,000 CELLS IN HUMAN BODY
- 186,282 MPS SPEED OF LIGHT
- 100,000,000,000,000,000,000,000,000,000,000,000,000,000,000,000,000,000,000,000,000,000,000,000,000,000,000,000 ATOMS IN THE UNIVERSE
- 1,390,000,000,000,000,000,000 H20 MOLECULES IN A DROP OF WATER

More On Powers

Venn Diagram - Advanced

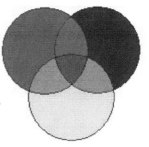

Venn diagrams are used for sorting things into categories.

For example:

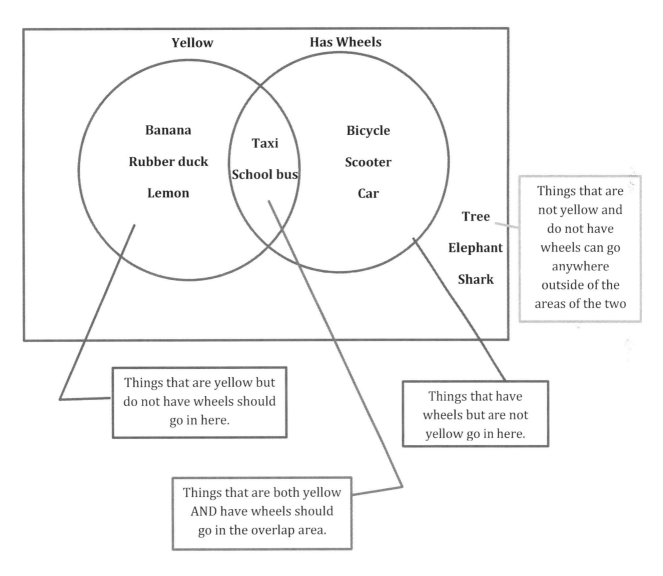

In math, we call these circles "**Sets**". They represent the different categories into which things, numbers, or events can be sorted.

Advanced Venn Diagrams

Drills:

Sort the following list of items into the Venn diagram.

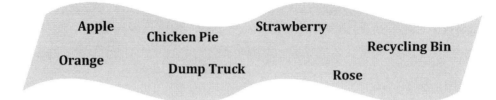

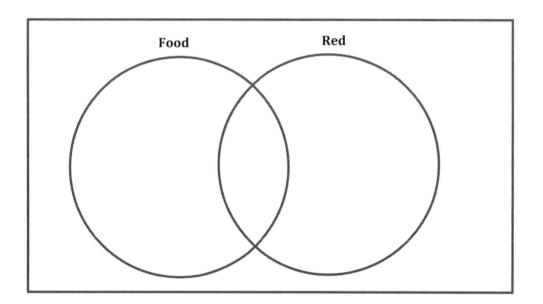

Use the same list above and sort them again into the following categories.

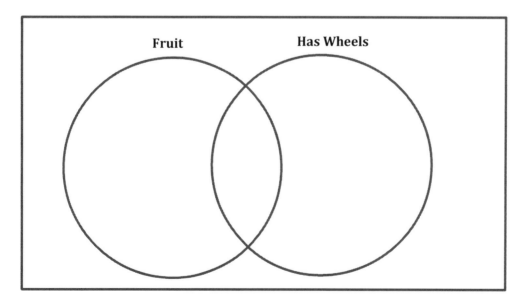

Notice how there is no item in the overlap of the two circles? Because there are no fruits with wheels!

When the two sets have nothing to do with each other, or cannot happen at the same time, we say that they are "mutually exclusive".

Name three more pairs of mutually exclusive sets:

_____ and _____

_____ and _____

_____ and _____

Advanced Venn Diagrams

Use the pictures below and sort the items into the following Venn diagram.

Are these sets mutually exclusive? _____

Sort the following numbers: 3, 5, 6, 8, 9, 12, 15, 16, 25, 42, 64, 81

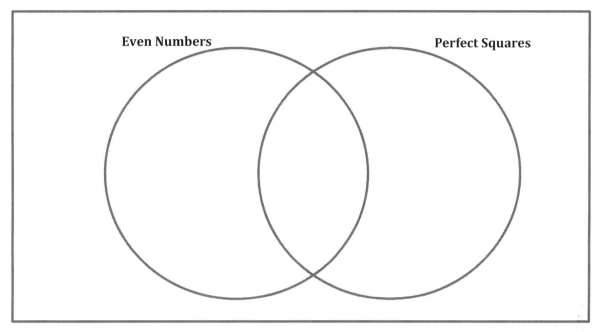

Are these sets mutually exclusive? _____

List all numbers between 2 to 25 and sort into the following Venn diagram.

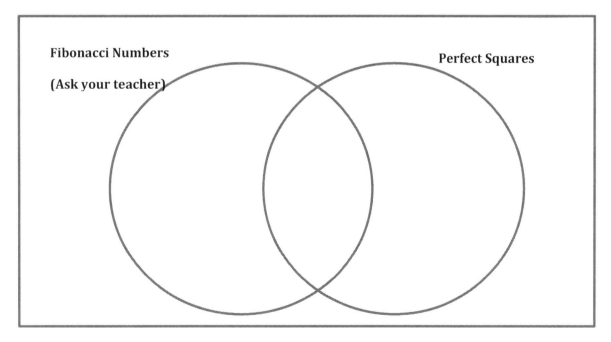

Are these sets mutually exclusive? _____

Advanced Venn Diagrams

Venn diagrams can also be used to sort three different categories. It will look something like this:

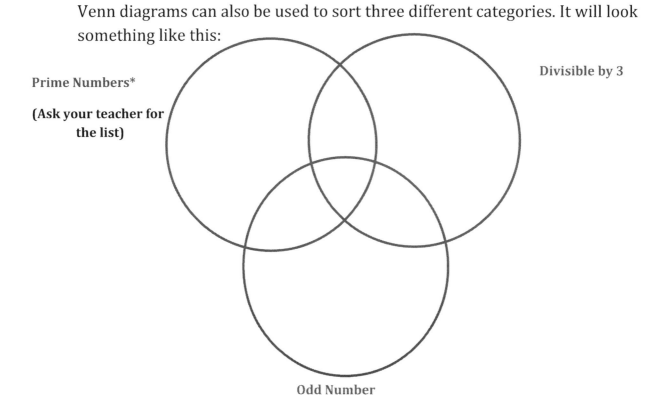

How many different areas are there is the 3-circle Venn Diagram?

Sort all numbers from 1 to 30:

1	2	3	4	5	6	7	8	9	10
11	12	13	14	15	16	17	18	19	20
21	22	23	24	25	26	27	28	29	30

1) The diagram below shows the classes students are taking.

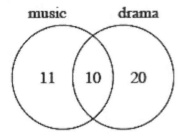

How many students are taking drama?

2) The diagram below shows the attributes of flowers in a flower shop.

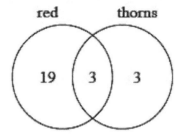

How many flowers only had thorns?

3) The diagram below shows the pets students in a class owned.

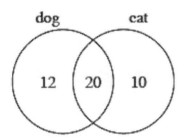

How many people had a dog?

4) The diagram below shows the sports people watched.

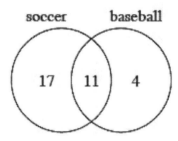

How many people watched baseball?

5) The diagram below shows the drinks people consumed at the football game.

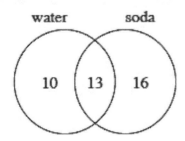

How many people drank water?

6) The diagram below shows the gender of students siblings.

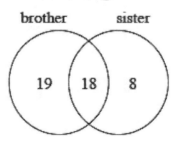

How many students had a sister?

Advanced Venn Diagrams

The diagram below shows the different places students had been in the last year. Water Park (W), Fair (F) and Zoo(Z). Use the diagram to answer the questions.

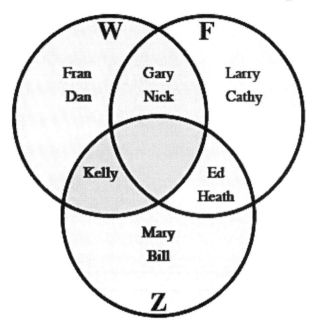

1) How many people had been to the water park? _____

2) How many people had been to the fair? _____

3) How many people had been to the zoo? _____

4) How many people had ONLY been to the water park? _____

5) How many people had ONLY been to the fair? _____

6) How many people had ONLY been to the zoo? _____

The beautiful Venn Diagram puzzle on the next page was created by our good friend **Dr. Gord! Hamilton (aka "Mr. Pickle")**. He is a father of two children, a mathematician, and designer of puzzles and board games. There is nothing the Doctor enjoys more than stumping students and having them stump him.

Dr. Gord is a master creator of beautiful puzzles, games and riddles to introduce students into tough problem solving activities. Problem solving is the primary reason we teach mathematics. Children deserve tough, beautiful puzzles, and Mr. Pickle is amazing at making them. For more from Dr. Gord! See www.mathpickle.com

The CRAZY 5-Category Venn Diagram
By Mr. Pickle (aka Dr. Gord!)

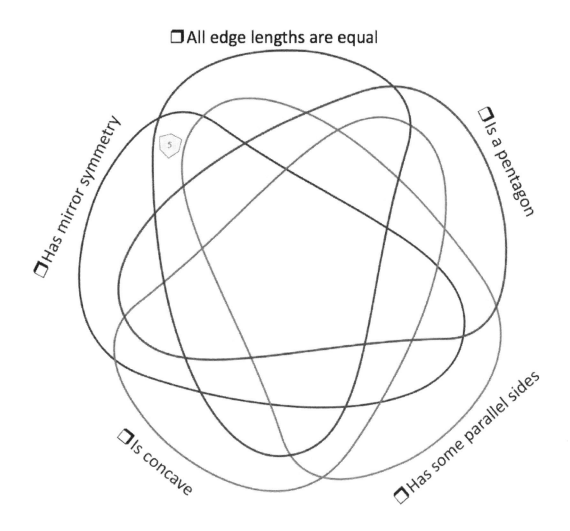

INSTRUCTIONS

Choose a polygon from the other page. Try to figure out where it goes. If I haven't made a mistake there should be one polygon in each region, but I *have* made a mistake because there are more polygons than regions to put them in. Help me out; find my mistakes.

PS. Edge lengths are equal unless they look really unequal.

Advanced Venn Diagrams

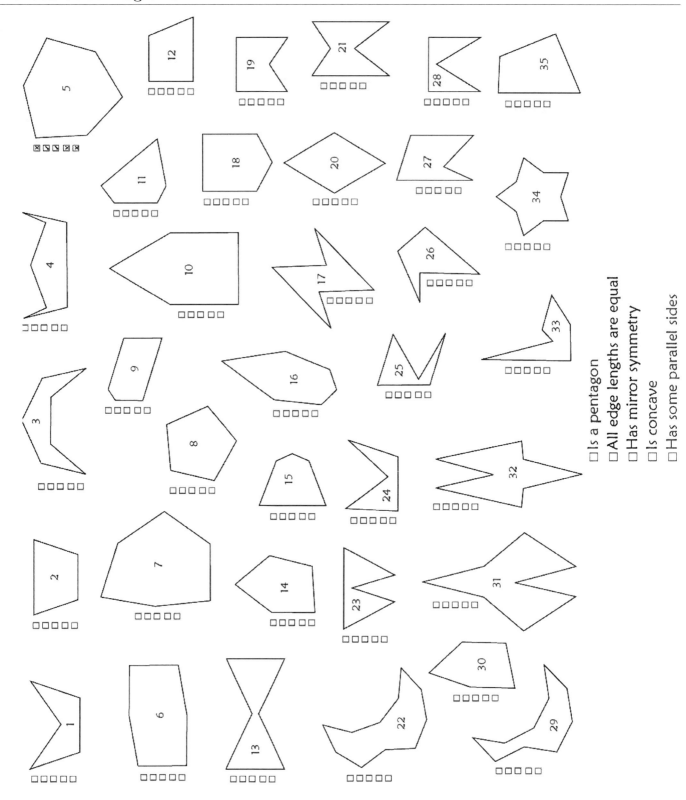

DEFINITIONS
Polygon – A closed geometrical figure where all edges are straight.
Pentagon – A 5-sided polygon

A shape is **Concave** if two points can be found inside it that the line that connects them passes outside the shape.

A shape is **Convex** if the line that connects ANY two points inside it, will always be inside the shape.

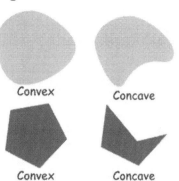

LAST ONE FOR YOU
- Look at the Venn Diagram below and study it carefully
- How many different areas does it have?
- Why do the "Have Fins" and the "Have Legs" circles do not touch one another?
- Add 5 more animals to the diagram placing them where they belong.

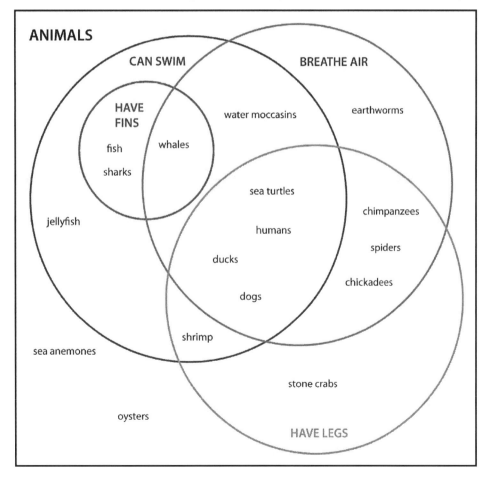

Class Activity: Animal Algebra 2

$\square$ + $\square$ = 12

$\triangle$ + $\bigcirc$ = 12

$\bigcirc$ + $\square$ = 13

Answer: $\square$ $\bigcirc$ $\triangle$

$\triangle$ + $\triangle$ + $\square$ = 11

$\square$ + $\bigcirc$ = 16

$\bigcirc$ + $\bigcirc$ = 22

Answer: $\square$ $\bigcirc$ $\triangle$

$\bigcirc$ + $\bigcirc$ + $\bigcirc$ + $\bigcirc$ = 16

$\square$ + $\bigcirc$ = 12

$\triangle$ + $\square$ = 14

Answer: $\square$ $\bigcirc$ $\triangle$

$$\square + \square + \square = 18$$
$$\triangle + \triangle + \bigcirc = 19$$
$$\bigcirc + \square = 11$$

Answer: $\square$ $\bigcirc$ $\triangle$

$$\bigcirc + \triangle - \square = 4$$
$$\square + \bigcirc = 12$$
$$\bigcirc + \triangle = 9$$

Answer: $\square$ $\bigcirc$ $\triangle$

$$\bigcirc + \triangle + \bigcirc + \triangle = 20$$
$$\square + \bigcirc = 13$$
$$\triangle + \square = 7$$

Answer: $\square$ $\bigcirc$ $\triangle$

Animal Algebra

$$\bigcirc + \bigcirc + \bigcirc = 15$$
$$\triangle + \bigcirc + \square = 21$$
$$\bigcirc + \square = 14$$

Answer: $\square \ \bigcirc \ \triangle$

$$\triangle + \square = 14$$
$$\triangle + \square + \square = 25$$
$$\bigcirc - \triangle = 5$$

Answer: $\square \ \bigcirc \ \triangle$

$$\square + \bigcirc + \bigcirc + \bigcirc = 15$$
$$\triangle + \bigcirc = 10$$
$$\bigcirc + \square + \bigcirc + \square = 14$$

Answer: $\square \ \bigcirc \ \triangle$

ALGEBRA and VARIABLES

Until now we only worked with numbers, concentrating on mastering our ARITHMETIC, the oldest and most elementary branch of mathematics. It consists of the **study of numbers**, and the operations between them—addition, subtraction, multiplication and division.

We are now gently moving into ALGEBRA, the study of mathematical symbols and the rules for manipulating them. In fact you HAVE seen algebra already whenever you solved an EQUTION like this one:

$\square + 3 = 5$. If your answer was 2, you are absolutely right! If you put 2 in the box, the two sides of the equation are equal to one another, so 2 is the correct solution. In mathematics we prefer not to use "box", and instead use a letter, typically the letter X.

For example, try to solve the equation: $X+3=5$. If your answer is 2, you are absolutely right! If you replace the X with the number 2, the two sides of the equation are equal to one another, so 2 is the correct solution. Observe that X and the box are really the same thing. X is just a placeholder for some number.

Before we continue let us make sure we all speak proper algebraic language:

VARIABLE – A letter that is a placeholder for a number (like "box" used to be).

EQUATION – A mathematical sentence that looks like **"Left Hand Side = Right Hand Side"**. We call it an equation because it has an EQUAL SIGN in the middle.

A. Solve for the given variable

1. $G = 9 + 6$ G = _____
2. $X + 5 = 18$ X = _____
3. $13 = K + 6$ K = _____
4. $J + 15 = 38$ J = _____
5. $G - 19 = 6$ G = _____
6. $X + 5 = 100$ X = _____
7. $G + G = 16$ G = _____
8. $17 - X = 3$ X = _____
9. $G+G+G = 24$ G = _____
10. $X+X-7=15$ X = _____
11. $X+X+7=15$ X = _____
12. $X+X=4*15$ X = _____
13. $G+G+G=9*6-12$ G = _____
14. $X+X+1=X+11$ X = _____
15*. $X+5=9-4+X$ X = _____
16*. $X+1=5+X$ X = _____

Introduction To Algebra

Four Dice: ☐ ☐ ☐ ☐

Make all the numbers from 0 to 20 by using these four numbers ONLY. You MUST use each of the numbers once. You may use +, -, ×, ÷, and also POWERS.

0=   5=   10=   15=

1=   6=   11=   16=

2=   7=   12=   17=

3=   8=   13=   18=

4=   9=   14=   19=

                            20=

Student Handbook - Level 3D

Four Dice: ☐ ☐ ☐ ☐

Make all the numbers from 0 to 20 by using these four numbers ONLY. You MUST use each of the numbers once. You may use +, -, ×, ÷, and also POWERS.

0=   5=   10=   15=

1=   6=   11=   16=

2=   7=   12=   17=

3=   8=   13=   18=

4=   9=   14=   19=

                                    20=

Three Dice: ☐ ☐ ☐

3 and 4 Dice Game

Make all the numbers from 0 to 20 by using these three numbers ONLY. You MUST use each of the numbers once. You may use +, -, ×, ÷, and also POWERS.

0=	5=	10=	15=
1=	6=	11=	16=
2=	7=	12=	17=
3=	8=	13=	18=
4=	9=	14=	19=
			20=

Student Handbook - Level 3D

Three Dice:

Make all the numbers from 0 to 20 by using these three numbers ONLY. You MUST use each of the numbers once. You may use +, -, ×, ÷, and also POWERS.

0=   5=   10=   15=

1=   6=   11=   16=

2=   7=   12=   17=

3=   8=   13=   18=

4=   9=   14=   19=

                              20=

MATH OLYMPIAD TRAINER SETS

Problem Set A1

1. Add up the following numbers. Think about what might be a smart way of doing it:

a. $1 + 2 + 3 + 4 + 5 + 6 + 7 + 8 + 9$

b. $4 + 6 + 8 + 10 + 12 + 14 + 16$

c. $1 + 3 + 5 + 7 + 9 + 11 + 13$

d. $5 + 8 + 11 + 14 + 17 + 20 + 23 + 26 + 29 + 32$

2. Complete each sequence:

a. 3, 5, 7, 9, ___, ___

b. 20, 17, 14, 11, ___, ___

c. 3, 6, 12, 24, ___, ___

d. 10, 13, 12, 15, 14, 17, 16, ___, ___

e. 1, 1, 2, 3, 5, 8, 13, ___, ___

f. 3, 4, 6, 9, 13, ___, ___

g. 2, 7, 8, 13, 14, 19, 20, ___, ___

h. Make one of your own and ask your friends to solve

3. Moshe is 8 years old and his mother is 20 years older than he is. How old will his mother be 7 years from now?

   What will be the difference between their ages 7 years from now?

4. Nona lives on the 4th floor of an apartment building. To get from one floor to the next one she needs to climb 11 stairs. How many stairs does she need to climb in order to get her dog Gordon, who ran up to the 10th floor?

5. *Freddie the frog fell into a well. The well is 10 meters high. Every day Freddie climbs up 5 meters, but at night when he falls asleep he slips back down 3 meters.

   How long will it take Freddie to get out of the well?

Set A2

1. Five years from now Estella will be 7 years older than her sister. Today Estella is 10. How old is her sister today?

2. Aidan drew 8 trees in a row like this:

   He then decided to draw 3 flowers between every two trees. How many flowers will he need to draw altogether?

3. Add up the following numbers. Think about what might be a smart way of doing it:

   a. 1 + 2 + 3 + 4 + 5 + 6 + ……….. + 16 + 17 + 18 + 19

   b. 1 + 2 + 3 + 4 + 5 + 6 + ……….. + 16 + 17 + 18 + 19 + 20

4. Yelena's has a beautiful cuckoo clock that strikes 1 time at 1 o'clock, twice at 2 o'clock, 3 times at 3 o'clock, and so on. How many times will the clock strike between 2:30 in the afternoon and 11:30 at night?

5. It takes 4 minutes to saw a log into 3 pieces. How long will it take to saw the log into 6 pieces? THINK CAREFULLY (this is not as easy as it looks)!

Math Olympiad Trainer

Set A3

1. How many marbles will be in the next pyramid?

   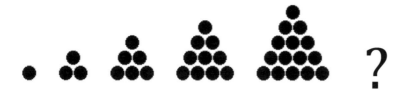

   The numbers 1, 3, 6, 10, 15, ... are called TRIANGULAR numbers. Can you see why?

2. Nancy says to her son Dylan: in 5 years I will be 23 years older than you. If Dylan is 7 years old today, how old is Nancy?

3. Can you give 10 candies to 4 children in a way that each child gets a different number of candies?

   Can you give 9 candies to 4 children in a way that each child gets a different number of candies? Explain.

4. Five gummy bears are sitting in a row, each gummy bear has 2 cats, and each of the cats has three hats. How many hats are there altogether?

5. The SUM of Yonatan's age and Danielle's age today is 19. In how many years will the sum of their ages be 29?

6. It takes Simon two minute to climb up the stairs of his building from one floor to the next. How long will it take him to climb from the 1st floor, where he lives, to the 5th floor, where his friend Maya lives?

Set A4

1. Find the next 3 members of the sequence:

   1, 4, 9, 16, 25, __, __, __

   The numbers 1, 4, 9, 16, 25 ... are called PERFECT SQUARES. Can you see why?

2. Right now it is 12 noon, and the two hands of the clock are one above the other. If you sit and look at the clock for the next 6 hours (until 6:00 PM), how many more times will there be where the two hands will be one above the other?

3. The sum of the ages of Moses, Lisa, Isaac, and Ben is 114. What will be the sum of the ages of all four of them in 3 years?

   If Ben is 11 today, how old will he be when the sum of the ages is 130?

4. Five gummy bears are sitting in a row. We put two rabbits between each two gummy bears, and then we put 4 ice cream cones between each two rabbits. How many ice cream cones will we need?

5. Steven left home to play tennis at 1:30PM. It took him 20 minutes to get to the court, and another half an hour to warm up. The game started immediately after the warm-up and took two hours and 35 minutes. It took him another hour to get back home because he had to stop on the way to get a Slurpee. At what time did Steven get home?

Set A5

1. You make a square made of coins, and you use 7 coins for each side of the square. How many coins altogether do you need for making the square?

   Now you do the same thing, but instead of a square, you make an EQUILATERAL triangle (a triangle with 3 equal sides) with 7 coins on each side. How many coins will you need for making the triangle?

2. How many squares are there in this figure?

   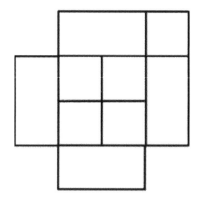

3. How many rectangles (of all sizes) are there in it?

   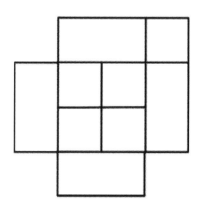

4. How many squares are there in this figure?

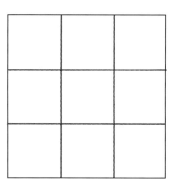

5. How many rectangles (of all sizes) are there in it?

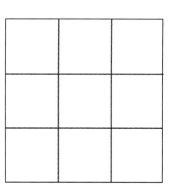

Set A6

1. Moses wanted to give his mother ONE flower from the three that he picked in the garden, and also ONE chocolate from the eight that he made in cooking class. How many different combinations are there for him to choose from (for example, the yellow flower and the moon-shaped chocolate is one combination)?

2. How many triangles (of all sizes) are there in this figure?

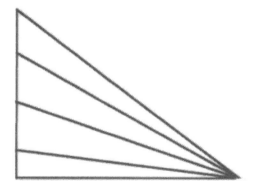

3. In how many ways can Albert, Betty and Charlie sit side by side?

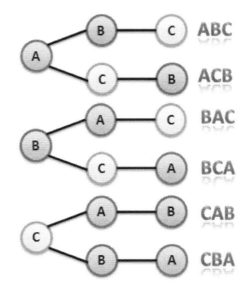

4. In how many ways can Abby, Bon, Cindy and Dorian sit side by side?

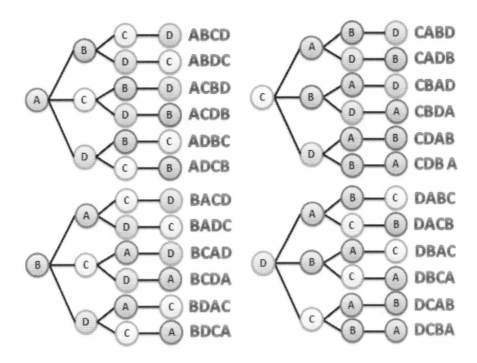

5. In how many ways can Ally, Baily, Cailey, Daly and Efus sit side by side?

Ancient Number Systems - Roman Numerals - Advanced

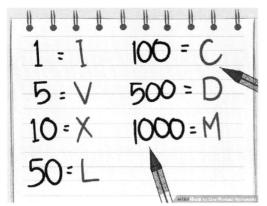

We have seen Roman Numerals in previous booklets, but now let us look at some of the bigger ones: L, C, D, and M, which represent 50, 100, 500 and 1000 (in that order).

When working with Roman Numerals there are a few rules we must follow. We have seen these rules before. Remember, for instance, that the number 9 is not written like this: VIIII, but instead like this: IX.

Rule 1: Start with the biggest digit and work your way towards the smallest one.
For example:
1984   = 1000 + 900 + 80 + 4
        = M + CM + LXXX + IV = MCMLXXXIV

Rule 2: When a symbol is followed by a smaller symbol, we add them
For example: VII = 5+1+1=7

Rule 3: When a symbol is followed by a larger symbol, we subtract them. For example: IV= 4.

Rule 4: We are not allowed to have the same symbol 4 times in a row

Rule 5: I can only be subtracted from V or X

Rule 6: X can only be subtracted from L or C

Rule 7: C can only be subtracted from D or M

1. Convert these numbers to standard form

(a) VII   (d) CML   (g) MCCXXX

(b) IX   (e) DCCLIII   (h) MMMDCCXIV

(c) XIV   (f) CLII

2. Convert from standard form to Roman numerals

(a) 19   (d) 590   (g) 543

(b) 999   (e) 1,685   (h) 1,111

(c) 3,778   (f) 976

3. Find the mistake in each one and correct it

(a) XIIII   (d) IVX   (g) IMX

(b) LLM   (e) XXXX   (h) XXXL

(c) XM   (f) VCIII

4. Calculate the following

(a) X-V   (d) X + CM

(b) M - DC   (e) V + IV + XXIII

(c) MDIX – CCCIV - VIII   (f) MCCXCIX - VIII

Introduction to Probability

In everyday life we hear people talk about chance. There are many ways that we hear people talk about it:

- I will **probably** pass this course if I do my homework.
- It will **likely** rain today.
- I may **possibly** go to the mall tonight.
- There is a **50-50 chance** that our team will win the hockey game tonight.

In mathematics, we usually use the word *"probability"* instead of the word *"chance"*. **Chance** and probability are used *in situations where the outcome is not necessarily known.* However, we often make decisions based on the likelihood or **probability** that *something may or may not occur.*

For example,

- I'll take my umbrella **if there is a good chance** it will rain today.
- It seems like a **100% chance** of a storm on the holidays.
- The **probability** of showers on Friday is **25%,** and on the weekend it is **99.9%**.
- The **probability** of winning the big prize in a lottery is less than **1:1 000 000**.

All the probabilities that we use will fall in the range from 0 to 1. A probability of ZERO (0%) means that the event CANNOT POSSIBLY OCCUR. A probability of ONE (100%) means that the event WILL HAPPEN FOR SURE.

We can represent this on a Probability line:

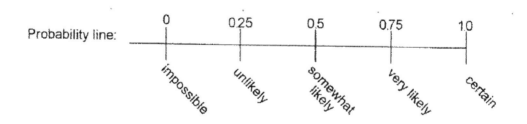

Can you think of something that has probability of ZERO to occur? _____

Can you think of something that has probability of ONE to occur? _____

All other probabilities are somewhere in between the 0% and the 100%.

Use the candy box to solve each problem.

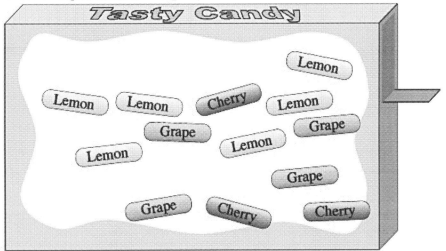

Answers

1. _____
2. _____
3. _____
4. _____
5. _____
6. _____
7. _____
8. _____
9. _____
10. _____

1) How many total pieces of candy are in the box?

2) What is the probability of selecting a cherry piece?

3) What is the probability of selecting a lemon piece?

4) What is the probability of selecting a grape piece?

5) If you picked 1 piece of candy out of the box which flavor would you have the highest probability of selecting?

6) Which flavor has the lowest probability of being selected?

7) If you picked a piece at random would you be more likely to select, a lemon piece or a cherry piece?

8) What is the probability of selecting either a cherry piece OR a grape piece?

9) Your friend wants either a cherry piece or a grape piece. If you picked a piece out randomly, which one would you have the highest probability of selecting?

10) If you ate 3 lemon pieces, 3 cherry pieces and 3 grape pieces, which flavor would you have the highest probability of selecting next?

Introduction to Probability

Use each diagram to solve the problems.

1) How many pieces are there total in the spinner?

2) If you spun the spinner 1 time, what is the probability it would land on a gray piece?

3) If you spun the spinner 1 time, what is the probability it would land on a black piece?

4) If you spun the spinner 1 time, what is the probability it would land on a white piece?

5) If you spun the spinner 1 time, what is the probability of landing on either a white piece or a black piece?

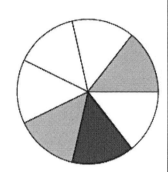

6) If you were to roll the dice one time what is the probability it will land on a 3?

7) If you were to roll the dice one time what is the probability it will NOT land on a 2?

8) If you were to roll the dice one time, what is the probability of it landing on an even number?

9) How many shapes are there total in the array?

10) If you were to select 1 shape at random from the array, what is the probability it will be a circle?

11) If you were to select 1 shape at random from the array, what shape do you have the greatest probability of selecting?

12) Which shape has a 32% chance (8 out of 25) of being selected?

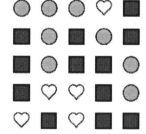

Answers

1. _____
2. _____
3. _____
4. _____
5. _____
6. _____
7. _____
8. _____
9. _____
10. _____
11. _____
12. _____

A. A jar contains 3 red, 14 brown, 1 white, 28 yellow, and 4 blue marbles. One marble is drawn at random. Find the probability of each event below as a simplified fraction:

1. P(red or yellow) = _____
2. P(green) = _____
3. P(white) = _____
4. P(not blue) = _____
5. P(brown, white, or blue) = _____

6. P(not green) = _____
7. P(yellow or brown) = _____
8. P(not yellow or blue) = _____
9. P(red) = _____
10. P(not yellow or brown) = _____

B. A fair die is rolled. Find the probability of each event below and express it as a simplified fraction.

11. P(1) = _____
12. P(a composite number) = _____
13. P(an even number) = _____
14. P(1, 2, or 3) = _____
15. P(not a 2) = _____

16. P(not an even number) = _____
17. P(3 or 4) = _____
18. P(not 2 or 5) = _____
19. P(8) = _____
20. P(a number less than 10) = _____

C. A spinner is divided into 10 equal sections. 4 sections are pink, 2 are black, 1 is silver, 1 is gold, and 2 are white. Find the probability of each spin below and express each as a decimal.

21. P(white) = _____
22. P(black) = _____
23. P(gold) = _____
24. P(silver or gold) = _____
25. P(not pink) = _____

26. P(not pink or silver) = _____
27. P(pink, black, or white) = _____
28. P(not silver or white) = _____
29. P(purple) = _____
30. P(pink) = _____

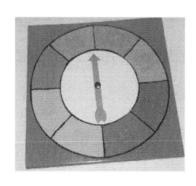

Introduction to Probability

Let us examine probability by doing an *experiment*. We will toss a fair die. We can say "fair" because there is an equal chance of the die falling on each of the six sides. By yourself or with a partner roll a die 30 times and record in the chart below the number of times each side faces up.

Number of dots on face	1	2	3	4	5	6	Total number of rolls:
Tally							
Number of times face was up							30

Use the data you collected to answer the following questions:

➢ Did you roll each of the 6 numbers at least once? _____

➢ Did you expect to see all 6 numbers? Why? _____

➢ Did one number come up more frequently than the others? Which one? _____

➢ Did you expect one number to come up more frequently than the rest? Why?

_____

➢ If we did this all over again, would we get the exact same results? Why?

_____

➢ Calculate the fraction of the rolls that were 1's, 2's, 3's, 4's, 5's, and 6's:

Fraction of 1s = $\dfrac{\text{total number of 1s rolled}}{\text{total number of rolls}}$ =

Fraction of 2s = $\dfrac{\text{total number of 2s rolled}}{\text{total number of rolls}}$ =

Fraction of 3s = $\dfrac{\text{total number of 3s rolled}}{\text{total number of rolls}}$ =

Fraction of 4s = $\dfrac{\text{total number of 4s rolled}}{\text{total number of rolls}}$ =

Fraction of 5s = $\dfrac{\text{total number of 5s rolled}}{\text{total number of rolls}}$ =

Fraction of 6s = $\dfrac{\text{total number of 6s rolled}}{\text{total number of rolls}}$ =

COINS

When a coin is tossed the outcome may be a *head (H)*, or a *tail (T)*. If the coin is "fair" then there is a 50-50 chance (meaning same probability) of coming up Heads as there is of coming up Tails.

Heads:

Tails:

Let us do an experiment: Toss each of the three coins TEN times and record in the chart below the number of times you tossed a head and the number of times a tail.

	Heads	Tails	No. of flips
Nickel			10
Dime			10
Quarter			10

What did you expect to see before you started flipping the coins? Is this what you actually saw when you counted the heads and the tails? Why do you think that is?

_____
_____
_____
_____

Pixels

Rules:

- Find and shade in squares from the hints given
- Number on each column/ row shows the number of shaded squares in that column/row
- Each number represent a chain of connecting squares
- If there are two or more numbers, it indicates a break (at least of one space) between the connecting chains
- Shade or color in the solution squares to reveal a message or picture

Easy Puzzles

Intermediate Puzzles

Color all empty (non-shaded) squares blue and all solution (shaded) squares black.

	2	4	2 3	6	6	6	4	2	4	6
0										
0										
4 1										
6 2										
2 7										
10										
6 2										
4 1										
0										
0										

	3	1 1 1	1 1 1	2	10	1 1 1	1 1 2	1	1	0
1										
1 1										
1 1										
1 1										
2										
4										
1 3										
1 1 1 1										
2 1 1										
2										

Color all empty (non-shaded) squares yellow and all solution (shaded) squares red.

	0	5	2 2	5 2	7	2 5	2 7	1 8	7	5
2										
2										
2 1 2										
4 4										
1 7										
1 7										
1 7										
2 6										
7										
2 2										

	2 3	1 1 3	1 5	1 2 2	1 8	5 1 2	2 6	4 1 2	8	5
2 3										
1 1 3										
1 5										
1 2 2										
1 8										
5 1 2										
2 6										
4 1 2										
8										
5										

Inroduction to Probability

Sudoku 8x8

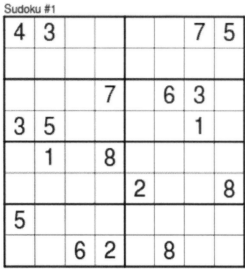

Sudoku #5

		2						
			8	3	6	2		
5	1							
	8							
	4		6					8
			2			6	5	
		4		7				3

Sudoku #6

7			6			1	4	
		3		6				
1		8						2
			4			7		
				8			5	
	1				2			
3		7						

Sudoku #7

	2		6			1		4
		3	1			2		
				5	7			
			5					
1						3	7	
	5	2		3		8		
		6						

Sudoku #8

	4		1					
7		2						
				6				8
					5			2
		5					7	4
2		6						
	3		5			8		
			8	4				

Inroduction to Probability

Inky 4x4

Inky #9

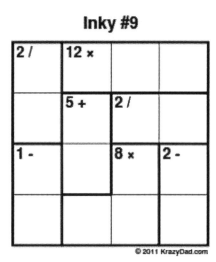

Inky #10

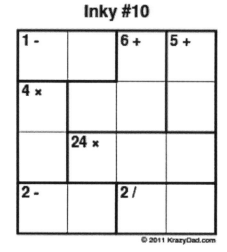

Inky #11

Inky #12

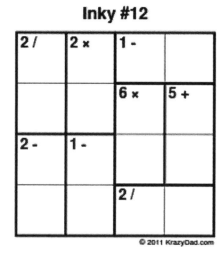

108 Renert's Bright Minds™ - August 9, 2020

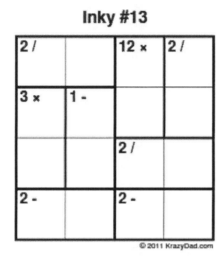

Inky 5x5

Inky #1
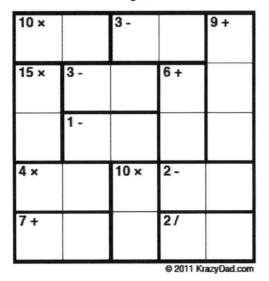

Inky #2
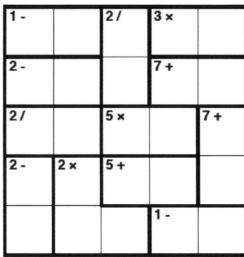

Inky #3
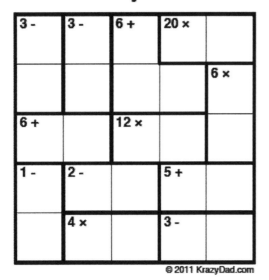

Inky #4
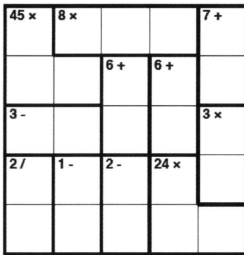

Inky #5

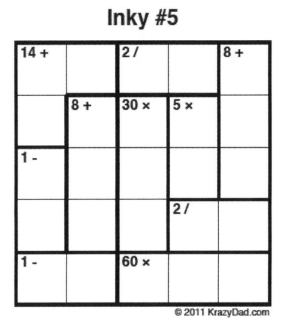

Inky #6

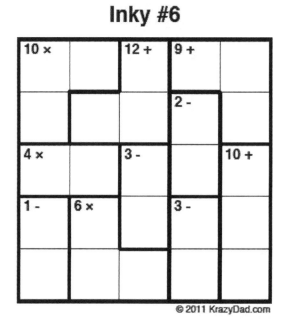

Inky #7

Inky #8

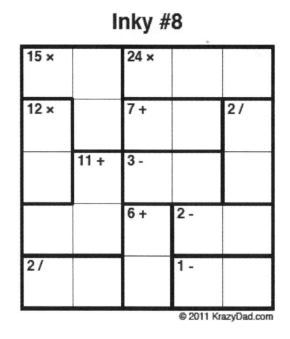

Inroduction to Probability

IXL Grade 3 Activities appropriate for level 3D

Numbers and comparing
A.7 Roman numerals I, V, X, L, C, D, M
A.13 Multi-step inequalities

Equations and variables
O.1 Identify equations
O.2 Solve for the variable
O.3 Write variable equations to represent word problems

Time
T.11 Convert between hours and fractions of hours
T.12 Reading schedules - 12-hour time
T.13 Reading schedules - 24-hour time
T.14 Timelines

Data and graphs
U.1 Objects on a coordinate plane
U.2 Coordinate planes as maps
U.3 Graph points on a coordinate plane
U.6 Interpret line plots
U.7 Create line plots
U.10 Interpret line graphs
U.11 Create line graphs
U.14 Venn diagrams with three circles

Units of measurement
V.1 Read a thermometer

V.2 Reasonable temperature
V.3 Which metric unit of length is appropriate?
V.4 Compare and convert metric units of length
V.5 Which metric unit of mass is appropriate?
V.6 Compare and convert metric units of mass
V.7 Which metric unit of volume is appropriate?
V.8 Compare and convert metric units of volume
V.9 Conversion tables

Geometry
W.5 Lines, line segments and rays
W.6 Angles greater than, less than or equal to a right angle
W.7 Acute, obtuse and right triangles
W.8 Scalene, isosceles and equilateral triangles
W.9 Reflection, rotation and translation
W.10 Similar and congruent

Geometric measurement
X.7 Volume

Equivalent fractions
Z.1 Find equivalent fractions using area models
Z.2 Graph equivalent fractions on number lines
Z.3 Find equivalent fractions
Z.4 Select equivalent fractions
Z.5 Reduce fractions to lowest terms

IXL Grade 4 appropriate for the 3D level

Variable expressions
G.1 Write variable expressions
G.2 Write variable expressions: word problems
G.3 Evaluate variable expressions
G.4 Write variable equations to represent word problems
G.5 Solve variable equations

Data and graphs
L.1 Read a table
L.2 Interpret line graphs
L.3 Create line graphs

L.4 Interpret bar graphs
L.5 Create bar graphs
L.6 Interpret line plots
L.7 Create line plots
L.8 Frequency charts
L.9 Stem-and-leaf plots
L.10 Circle graphs
L.11 Choose the best type of graph

Units of measurement

IXL Recommended Exercises

N.1 Choose the appropriate metric unit of measure
N.2 Compare and convert metric units of length
N.3 Compare and convert metric units of mass
N.4 Compare and convert metric units of volume

Time

O.1 Convert time units
O.2 Add and subtract mixed time units
O.3 Fractions of time units
O.4 Elapsed time
O.5 Find start and end times: multi-step word problems
O.6 Convert between 12-hour and 24-hour time
O.7 Time zones - 12-hour time
O.8 Time zones - 24-hour time
O.9 Transportation schedules - 12-hour time
O.10 Transportation schedules - 24-hour time
O.11 Time patterns

Geometric measurement

Q.6 Volume

Equivalent fractions

S.1 Find equivalent fractions using area models
S.2 Graph equivalent fractions on number lines
S.3 Equivalent fractions
S.4 Fractions with denominators of 10, 100, and 1000
S.5 Patterns of equivalent fractions
S.6 Reduce fractions to lowest terms

Probability and statistics

W.1 Calculate probability
W.2 Make predictions

IXL GRADE 5 Activities appropriate for the 3D Level

Place values and number sense

A.1 Place values
A.2 Convert between place values
A.3 Compare numbers up to millions
A.4 Word names for numbers
A.5 Roman numerals
A.6 Rounding
A.7 Even or odd: arithmetic rules

Fractions and mixed numbers

I.1 Show fractions: fraction bars
I.2 Show fractions: area models
I.3 Fractions review
I.4 Understanding fractions: word problems
I.5 Mixed numbers
I.6 Fractions of a number
I.7 Fractions of a number: word problems
I.8 Arithmetic sequences with fractions
I.9 Geometric sequences with fractions
I.10 Round mixed numbers

Fraction equivalence and ordering

J.1 Find equivalent fractions using area models
J.2 Graph equivalent fractions on number lines
J.3 Equivalent fractions
J.4 Patterns of equivalent fractions
J.5 Write fractions in lowest terms
J.6 Graph and compare fractions on number lines
J.7 Compare fractions
J.8 Compare fractions and mixed numbers
J.9 Order fractions with like denominators
J.10 Order fractions with like numerators
J.11 Order fractions

Mixed operations

M.1 Add, subtract, multiply and divide whole numbers
M.2 Add, subtract, multiply and divide whole numbers: word problems
M.3 Write numerical expressions
M.4 Evaluate numerical expressions

Problem solving

N.1 Multi-step word problems
N.2 Word problems with extra or missing information
N.3 Guess-and-check problems
N.4 Find the order
N.5 Use Venn diagrams to solve problems

N.6 Price lists

Patterns and sequences
O.1 Find the next shape in a repeating pattern
O.2 Complete a repeating pattern
O.3 Make a repeating pattern
O.4 Find the next row in a growing pattern of shapes
O.5 Complete an increasing number sequence
O.6 Complete a geometric number sequence
O.7 Use a rule to complete a number sequence
O.8 Number sequences: word problems
O.9 Number sequences: mixed review

Coordinate plane
P.1 Objects on a coordinate plane
P.2 Graph points on a coordinate plane
P.3 Coordinate planes as maps

Variable expressions
Q.1 Write variable expressions
Q.2 Write variable expressions: word problems
Q.3 Evaluate variable expressions
Q.4 Write variable equations: word problems
Q.5 Solve equations with whole numbers

Time
T.1 Convert time units
T.2 Add and subtract mixed time units
T.3 Elapsed time
T.4 Find start and end times: word problems

Two-dimensional figures
V.1 Is it a polygon?
V.2 Number of sides in polygons
V.3 Regular and irregular polygons
V.4 Parallel, perpendicular and intersecting lines
V.5 Types of angles

Three-dimensional figures
X.1 Identify three-dimensional figures
X.2 Count vertices, edges and faces
X.3 Nets of three-dimensional figures
X.4 Three-dimensional figures viewed from different perspectives

Geometric measurement
Y.1 Perimeter
Y.2 Area of squares and rectangles
Y.3 Area and perimeter of figures on grids
Y.4 Use area and perimeter to determine cost
Y.5 Volume

IXL Recommended Exercises

Assessment Test for end of 3D Level

1.	Use mental calculation.	
	(a) 34 + 28 = (b) 62 – 37 =	[4]
	(c) 600 x 5 = (d) 3600 ÷ 9 =	[4]
2.	Fill in the blanks.	
	(a) 5 m – 3 m 45 cm = _____ m _____ cm	[2]
	(b) 3408 m = _____ km _____ m	[2]
	(c) 3 kg 250 g – 1 kg 600 g = _____ kg _____ g	[2]
	(d) 3 L 6 ml = _____ ml	[2]
	(e) 4 L 400 ml + 680 ml = _____ L _____ ml	[2]
	(f) 5 h 10 min – 3 h 25 min = _____ h _____ min	[2]
	(g) 1 year 8 months = _____ months	[2]
	(h) 30 days = _____ weeks _____ days	[2]

3.	A melon is 5 times as heavy as an orange. If the orange weighs 450 g, find the weight of the melon. Give your answer in kilograms and grams.	[5]
4.	John took 2 h 40 min to paint his room. He finished at 1:30 p.m. What time did he begin painting his room?	[5]
5.	String A is 85 cm long. String B is twice as long. String C is 30 cm shorter than string B. How long is string C? Give your answer in meters and centimeters.	[5]

6. This bar graph shows David's savings for five months.

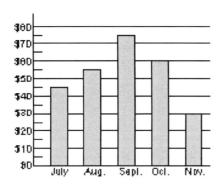

Use the graph to answer the following questions.

(a) David saved _____ in August. [2]

(b) He saved the least money in _____. [2]

(c) In _____ he saved twice as much as in November. [2]

(d) He saved _____ more in October than in July. [2]

7. Find the missing numbers for the top or bottom of the fractions.

(a) $\dfrac{2}{3} = \dfrac{\Box}{12} = \dfrac{4}{\Box}$ (b) $\dfrac{6}{18} = \dfrac{\Box}{6} = \dfrac{1}{\Box}$ [4]

8. Circle the larger fraction.

(a) $\dfrac{4}{5}$ $\dfrac{4}{9}$ (b) $\dfrac{2}{3}$ $\dfrac{5}{6}$ [2]

9. Peter, Sam, and Mary shared a pizza. Peter and Sam each had $\frac{2}{5}$ of the pizza. How much pizza did Mary have? **[4]**

10. Melissa ate $\frac{2}{6}$ of a pie. Sara ate $\frac{1}{2}$ of the pie.

    (a) Who ate a bigger portion of the pie? **[2]**

    (b) How much pie was left over? **[2]**

11.

    75 cm

    40 cm

    50 cm

    45 cm

    (a) The perimeter of this figure in centimeters is _____ cm **[2]**

    (b) The perimeter in meters and centimeters

    is _____ m _____ cm **[2]**

    (c) The figure has _____ right angles. **[2]**

3D Final Assessment

12. The length of a rectangular field is 60 m and its width is 25 m. Sam ran around the field three times. How far did he run? [5]

13. The rectangle and the square have the same perimeter. The length of the rectangle is 6 cm, and its width is 2 cm. Find their areas.

6 cm

2 cm

(a) The area of the rectangle is _____. [3]

(b) The area of the square is _____. [2]

14. Mary made 465 rolls. She gave away 15 rolls and sold the rest at 6 for $1. How much money did she receive? [5]

[All rights reserved to www.singaporemath.com]

120   Renert's Bright Minds™ - August 9, 2020

HOMEWORK TRACKING

Homework Assignment

HOMEWORK TRACKING

Homework Assignment

HOMEWORK TRACKING

Homework Assignment

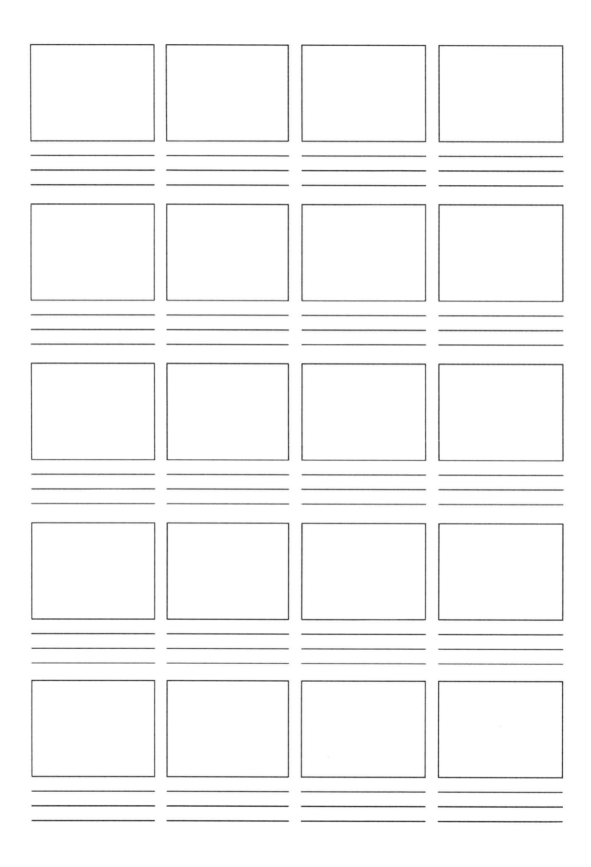

Marking Key - Guide to Parents and Markers

The reason we include a marking key at the end of each booklet is so students can tell in real time whether they understand the material and are getting the correct answers. Solving math problems without knowing if you are doing it correctly is time-wasteful, and even pointless. This is where you, the parent, can greatly help both your child, as well as the teacher.

How to do it right? Please follow these guidelines closely:

- Grab your favourite yellow highlighter.

- Place a checkmark ✓ with a pen beside any question the child gets correct.

- HIGHLIGHT with a yellow highlighter the question number of any question the child got wrong. If the question is unnumbered, you can highlight the wrong answer itself.

- Ask the child to go over their mistakes, and try to correct, to the best of their ability. If it is a careless error, the child should be able to find and correct it. If it is an error that stems from lack of understanding of how to solve the question, this is fine. We will explain the concept again to the child in class and guide him to the solution.

- We do not expect you to teach your child any of the mathematical concepts at home. This is our job, but it speeds us tremendously when the marking was done at home, so we can see very quickly where the child went wrong.

- Do NOT spoon feed solutions to your child or guide them too heavily. As instructors we always assume that a correct answer is one that the child worked out, and that if asked how they got it, they should be able to explain. Making many mistakes is part of the learning process and **there is nothing wrong with it**. As a parent you have to get very comfortable with your child making mistakes. You will speed your child up, however, by highlighting these mistakes and asking the child if they can correct them unassisted.

- Feel free to communicate with the instructor by jotting comments in the booklet and asking your child to show them to the instructor. For instance, you may write "really struggles with long division, but understands very well short division..." etc. Again, it helps our instructors a great deal in knowing what to zoom in on.

- Marking key is to use, not abuse. If the child starts copying answers wholesale and presents them as their own, explain to them how unproductive it is, and that they should not do it.

You can access the **3D digital marking key** at: https://bit.ly/33HcN2N

Solutions

Made in the USA
Middletown, DE
22 December 2021